MW00441836

FALSE PROFITS

"*False Profits* is a 'must read' for anyone even thinking about getting into multi-level marketing in any form. It's a real eye-opener that will serve anyone who is considering this form of enterprise."

> – John Renesch, Editor/Publisher
> *The New Leaders* business newsletter

"Bravo to Robert Fitzpatrick and Joyce K. Reynolds for having the insight and the courage to point out how perilously thin the line can be between 'prosperity consciousness' and old-fashioned selfishness and greed."

> – Laurence Shames, author
> *The Hunger for More* published by Random House

"...*False Profits* invites you to determine, examine or reaffirm your highest ideals for a life that is worth living as it points out the profound distinctions between an existence founded upon material success... and one that is dedicated to communal and spiritual vision."

FALSE PROFITS

Seeking Financial and Spiritual
Deliverance in Multi-Level Marketing
and Pyramid Schemes

Robert L. Fitzpatrick
Joyce K. Reynolds

Herald Press
Charlotte, NC

Herald Press
1235-E East Blvd. #101
Charlotte, NC 28203
Fax: (704) 334-0220
E-mail: FalsProfts@aol.com
World Wide Web: http://www.FalseProfits.com

Publisher's Cataloguing in Publication
(Prepared by Quality Books, Inc.)

Fitzpatrick, Robert L./Reynolds, Joyce K.
    False profits : seeking financial and spiritual deliverance in multi-level marketing and pyramid schemes / Robert L. Fitzpatrick, Joyce K. Reynolds. – [Rev. ed.]
        p. cm.
    Includes bibliographical references and index.
    Pre-assigned LCCN: 96-095149
    ISBN 0-9648795-1-4

    1. Multi-level marketing 2. Fraud–Florida–Case studies. 3. New Age movement
    I. Reynolds, Joyce K. II. Title

HF5415.126.F58 1997   658.8'4
                                        QBI95-20681

Acknowledgments

Robert L. Fitzpatrick

I thank my wife, Terry Thirion, for her conviction that the message of this book is valuable and needed. I thank my monthly dinner and support group friends for their interest and encouragement after reading the first chapters. I thank theater producer and writer, Burton Wolfe, for his gentle but firm urging to keep my word about publishing this book. I give special gratitude to counselor and author, Matthew Anderson, who told me not to let rejections discourage me from getting published. Friends Ed Greville and Steve Lanosa I thank for powerfully validating the book and inspiring me to put aside second thoughts. Personal friend and graphic designer, Shep Root, I thank for reminding me of my abilities for promoting and defending my heretical ideas.

I am especially grateful to those who came to my home for an emotional and confrontational critique of this book.

Joyce K. Reynolds

It never occurred to me that I would so enjoy being unable to tell where another's thoughts or words left off and mine began until I worked with Bob on this book. I am immensely grateful to have experienced this kind of respectful, creative collaboration.

Appreciation must also go to my dear sister, Judy, and her husband, John Morgan, for their ever-present love, support and gentle care of my soul. And, to their children, David, Richard and Alison, who not only add immeasurably to my life but who have done the honor of holding me in high esteem despite my often changing fortunes.

A million thanks must then be sent to my countless New York City pals for their ever continuing support with special gratitude to Nuala Byrne, B.J. Kaplan, Charles Mohacey and Cathy Wallach for their endless generosity and unconditional love.

Cover Art

Everything passes; pleasure,
glory, glitter, all that one boasts
about on this earth. It vanishes,
no matter what we do.

This message, written in French upon the pedestal and delivered by an unknown Franciscan artist nearly 300 years ago, is as true today as it was in the post Reformation environment of France when he created the original engraving.

Issuing in Latin from a human skull are words forebodingly imploring the reader to "Think your highest thought." Meanwhile an angel, overlooking a nobleman's prosperous estate, orders the deceased to "Now arise and approach the gate for your judgment."

The engraving, created in a time of great spiritual upheaval, addresses the age-old dichotomy of spirituality which is soulful and timeless and financial prosperity which is temporal and material. The artist sees the two worlds of spiritual salvation and material prosperity as separate and mutually exclusive domains. Today, prevailing beliefs treat financial prosperity as salvation itself or, at least, God's sign of spiritual deliverance.

This engraving is one of thousands of ancient renderings by unknown monks around the world that are being assembled and archived in a small monastery in Belgium. With diligence, patience and very little money, volunteers are preserving such works whose timeless messages are written in ink which is fading and on paper which is crumbling.

A portion of the revenue from this book is being contributed to support the preservation effort.

Contents

False Profits

Introduction

False Profits

"We're Looking For Five Exceptional Leaders..."

Aboard a plane heading for Kansas City, the attractive young woman sitting next to me turned to the person behind and asked, "I noticed you reading the classifieds earlier. Are you looking for work?"

"Yes, I am," said the occupant, a woman in her early twenties who seemed surprised but pleased that someone had taken an interest in her. "Actually, I've been looking for a job for quite some time. Why do you ask?"

"Well, I'm sort of in human resources for my company and we're looking for people right now."

"Really? What kind of a company is it?"

"Well, we represent over 200 environmentally friendly products."

"Really? That's terrific. I really believe in products that protect the environment."

"We're growing really fast now and expanding."

"That's great!"

"Would you like to talk about it when we get to Kansas City?"

"Well, sure, but I'm looking for work in Maine. That's where I live."

"Actually, we have an office in Maine. What's your schedule like tonight or tomorrow?"

"I'm busy all day tomorrow."

"Okay, let's get together this evening. It'll be fun."

"Great."

"Believe me, this is the opportunity of a lifetime. I can't wait to tell you all about it."

An elderly woman next to the job seeker commented, "It sounds like you've hit the lottery."

"Yeah, what luck!"

Yes, you might think so. Yet, without asking, I instinctively knew that this 'human resources' recruiter was not a human resources professional at all. She was not authorized to offer a 'job' of any kind to anyone. In fact, she did not even have a job herself.

She was an independent distributor plying her wares and looking for sub-distributors. Far from offering a job, she was seeking a financial investment from the young woman behind her. She was one of the modern day equivalents of the itinerant agent who sold stock certificates in promising – or more often bogus – companies to the naive, the gullible and the greedy on the Herman Melville, Mark Twain-style Mississippi steamboats.

This enthusiastic and helpful traveler was yet another recruiter of a multi-level or network marketing company (MLM) in which – through a pyramid-like commission structure – each distributor has the opportunity to gain override payments on sales of as many as six levels of sales reps below. Success in this business involves a ceaseless and boundless search for downliners on the commission feeding chain below, a practice which leads to the necessity for these types of open and constant business solicitations. The fellow traveler who was the target of her initiatives was, surprisingly, one of few people who had never before encountered an MLM or pyramid scheme. Her innocent and unguarded questions showed that she was not alert to this type of proposition.

This was to be her induction, her rite of passage into a whole new business genre. We can only imagine her reaction to later finding out from the recruiter that the initial 'job' offer she was so excited about would actually turn into a solicitation to invest. The distributor, like her many counterparts, would, undoubtedly, have wrapped such a clarification in a penetrating, highly seductive presentation of her company and its superior product . Such MLM pitches frequently include the tantalizingly presented potential for a $50,000 monthly income along with promises of personal freedom and independence, effortless lifetime annuities and early retirement, all within easy reach especially for those who have vision, talent and a love for people. And, it may well have worked on that un-informed, unemployed young woman from Maine as it has on countless millions of others. The story goes on.

On that occasion, I pretended not to hear. I feigned sleep as we awaited take-off. I avoided eye contact though I felt my traveling companion's hyperactive presence. Ultimately, conversation was unavoidable for I was proofreading this very manuscript. My papers provided her with an opening foray. After all, she was on a roll. One appointment was already made. She was undoubtedly thinking that this could be the day on which she would hit the jackpot with that one downliner who would set the world on fire resulting in her accruing benefits for the balance of her born days.

"Pyramid schemes and MLMs," I replied quietly when she inquired about the subject of my manuscript.

Thus began another close encounter with a true believer, an MLM proselyte. Once again I faced the challenge of speaking constructively about what I have studied, learned and concluded about this type of business. And, once again, I saw that information turned away because it disturbed the old get-rich-quick notion that has entrenched itself in the American mind.

After getting the gist of my theme, this enthusiastic recruiter suddenly found herself struggling for civility, all the while bristling with underlying defensiveness. I had attacked the bastion of her faith, the seat of her dream, her very path to success. And I was treading on America's most treasured, even sacrosanct doctrine – the right of each American to unlimited personal opportunity and the chance to become wealthy 'beyond one's wildest imaginings.'

So what if 99.9% fail at MLM, she countered. Certainly it was because they had not really tried. People fail at all kinds of businesses. In fact, most small businesses fail, she continued. Failure in MLM is clearly and only the responsibility of people who don't apply themselves.

Oh, she knew about MLM fraud and misleading promotions and recruitment. She volunteered knowledge of the 1990 Fund America, Inc. fiasco that swindled thousands of distributors across the country out of millions.[1] She had even lost $3,000 in that mess herself. She knew that the government had closed down Fund America as an illegal pyramid scheme resulting in the arrest of the president of the company – who later fled the country with millions in company funds – and the subsequent discovery that he was wanted for fraud in England.

Our believer had also been an Amway rep. She had paid for training and motivational tapes that were essentially about recruitment and manipulation, just another way to get money from the inexperienced and naive. And she knew all about the disreputable recruitment tactics of so many other MLMs. But *this* one was different, she insisted. After all, she was already a director – as if her current success was certain proof of this company's validity.

She went on. Yes, the founder of her company had been an executive in one of those misleading MLMs but he had seen the abuses and he had corrected them in his new company. Pointedly, I asked just how many people were needed in an individual distributor's downline to provide a sustainable monthly income. She said maybe a couple of hundred if all of them were consistent producers.

---

[1] Fund America, Inc. of Irvine, California, was an MLM buying club that attracted over 100,000 members nationwide, offering discounts on goods and services. In 1990, Florida law enforcement officials arrested president Robert T. Edwards on suspicion of criminal fraud. He was released on $1 million bail. The company was prevented from operating in some states and later declared bankruptcy. It was, subsequently, discovered that Edwards had taken $5.5 million in the form of salaries and bonuses and personally wired $11.3 million more to two mysterious overseas entities, one in Hong Kong, the other in the Netherlands.

Then I asked how many in her company presently had sustainable living incomes of $4,000 a month. Some were making over $50,000 a month, she replied tartly. Avoiding this obvious diversion, I pressed for the number of only those with middle class incomes of $4,000 a monthly.

Thousands, she said.

I noted that this would already indicate a collective downline of over a half million people in the U.S. in her company alone. Was that possible?

She pondered the figures briefly and, without the slightest loss of composure, said that she did not know the real number nor did she *care* to know. There was always opportunity and MLMs had barely begun to scratch the potential of the U.S. market. Anyone could make it if they just worked hard.

Now I couldn't resist going a little farther. Even at the risk of sounding like a small town Methodist cleric warning against the evils of money and city life, I mentioned the commercialization of personal relationships, the manipulation of friendships and the blatant misuse of family trust each of which so characterize the MLM industry.

Everything is commercial, she snapped, as if I had been asleep for the last 100 years. We are all always selling. That's life today, she huffed.

As for traditional jobs, vocations and professions, well, corporations only use people, she said. She herself had once worked for a company and calculated that it had only paid her 1% of what she had actually made for them. Those kinds of companies just suck your blood and then fire you when you hit 50, she declared.

Thus having regained the adrenaline rush she had experienced after securing a appointment with the job hopeful behind us, she told me that I was simply resisting the wave of the future. Really. Just look at MCI, the long distance phone carrier, which is going MLM. It's everywhere, she said. She was telling me?!

But, on she went. In MLM, you can make a fortune with virtually no up-front investment. Right. It's providing opportunity to millions of people who are being thrown out of corporate America. Hmm. It will, in fact, provide security when Social Security goes bankrupt. And, it will go bankrupt, she finished triumphantly! Well, who could argue that point?

And, as for regulation, well, the government should just stay out of MLM, she said. It was really the government that destroyed Fund America, Inc. and caused her to lose $3,000. If do-good government regulators had not gotten into it, Fund America would still be going and she would probably be good and rich by now. They had caused thousands to lose their money when they intervened, she railed as she gained momentum. She would rather see people take their own chances than lose their money for sure when the government closes down a company.

Somewhat caught up now, I noted that the government finds itself forced to intervene because pyramid schemes are structured to inevitably fail. They take money from those at the bottom and feed it to those at the top. I pointed out that the initial success of such businesses is an illusion. That eventually the base grows too large and is not sustainable. And that's why they are illegal. That's what the fraud is all about.

At this point, my passion began to dwindle as I was regretting my part in this discussion. As soon as the word fraud had slipped from my mouth, I realized that any further attempt at communication had collapsed if, indeed, it had ever had a chance.

Further, it was clear that our now totally defensive distributor had cast me in the role of a representative of that Fifth Column of negativity, government control, skepticism, cynicism and collectivism that she, in short, described as completely un-American. Thus, as the plane began its descent into Kansas City, she delivered her coup de grâce.

"I can live with risk, even failure," she said haughtily. "But, what I can't stand are dream busters, cynics who want nothing more than to kill other people's dreams." Her company, she said, offered the chance for the American dream to come true. I, on the other hand, simply offered nothing positive. Her last words.

The plane mercifully landed as I wondered if the young woman behind us had heard any of our discussion and if the appointment would be kept. Alas, the bogus human resources professional and the accused dream buster didn't bother to exchange business cards. We didn't even say good-bye.

Aftermath

Along with countless others that are taking place as this story is being read, this encounter demonstrates that the ubiquitous proponents of MLM are not easily evaded, ignored or rebutted. This new form of selling relies not on product or cash to build its portfolio but on human resources. Growth of the MLM must proceed not incrementally or one by one in the traditional business model but rather exponentially. One hundred are required to support one and ten thousand more to support the one hundred. Solicitations must always expand and accelerate. Momentum is the engine. Therefore, even flying high in the stratosphere, recruits must be found. It's the only way the MLM story can go on.

With mesmerizing promises of extraordinary and easily attainable wealth, assurances of personal freedom and happiness, MLM and pyramids are touted as answers to fearsome warnings of economic insecurity or even global chaos. Regularly offered are the irrefutable reminders that the only tools needed to build a successful downline, sales or participation team are as near as all of one's friends and relatives. Certainly, to avoid the fate of running afoul of an MLM or an illegal pyramid in America today seems nearly impossible.[2]

---

[2] So frequent and pervasive has the push for enrollments into illegal pyramid schemes become in American society that network television sitcom, *The Single Guy*, made it comic material for an episode in
continued on next page

While the paid media may bombard our subconscious, their seductions and influences are offered via print and electronics which we are free to avoid or turn off. MLM and illegal pyramids use no advertising nor have they any need for it. They simply walk in the front door in the guise of a friend, lover or brother-in-law. To withstand such individualized and intense enrollment efforts requires a strong sense of personal security.

At the very least, a savvy insight into the actual odds of success and a set of definitive questions are needed in order to make a free and intelligent choice. Faced with solicitations from friends or relatives, a level of fortitude and social skills is required that would test the limits of any personal relationships, especially those which are traditionally safe havens from commercial trade. In this context, it is no wonder that MLM evokes such powerful responses from blind allegiance to bitter contempt.

Burning with zeal, millions have joined the movement. A nearly equal number fail early and abandon the program. Their ranks, however, are quickly replenished by new draftees. For reasons that will be closely examined later in this book, almost no one who has been through the process can provide a coherent explanation of the experience other than to offer a painful admission of their own apparent insufficiency.

With vast numbers of people failing at enterprises convincingly portrayed as easily-mastered while offering enormous financial potential, it should not be surprising that a psychic pall of disillusionment and disappointment has fallen over millions of past participants. Far from a program that is unleashing

---

February, 1996. The concept required no explanation, the writers assuming correctly that most viewers are personally familiar with the phenomenon. The denial of the scheme's illegality and the deluded hopes of easy and quick money were made the stuff of laughter even as one of the regular characters was arrested and led off to jail at the show's end.

human potential and fulfilling dreams as the aforementioned traveling companion claimed, if we look, we will see a voracious organism that churns and manipulates believers of the American Dream. It leaves in its wake a trail of cynicism and disempowerment, no small wonder as recruits observe billions of dollars landing in the laps of tiny, elite groups at the top.

Our proselytizing travel companion prompted the recurring questions about the true income potential from MLM enterprises, the limits of their mathematical expansion and the legalities of and differences between MLM and pyramids. Where does the truth lie in these all too frequent and unavoidable solicitations? Certainly not in misleading sales openers like the one offered by our ersatz human resource recruiter. Definitely not in her exaggerated numbers about income potential or the success levels of MLMers. And, not in her revisionist history of the Fund America fraud. Yet, neither was there validity in the countering call for government regulation or the high-minded detachment from MLM's promise of wealth and happiness.

Eventually, clarification came with the realization that the mundane matters of pyramid structures, the promotional rhetoric and success levels of participants are insignificant sidelines to the main issue. MLM and the associated phenomenon of pyramid schemes are worth investigation and understanding because of the powerful spiritual and social messages they are espousing and for what their growth and expansion in America reveal about our lives.

What we need to focus on is the fact that the increasing influence of multi-level marketing is not based upon what is actually delivered to people in income or on the products that are sold in the marketplace. Indeed, the appalling failure rate of participants in MLM and the illogic and illegality of pyramid schemes would cause any reasonable person to wonder why anyone would enroll in such improbable ventures.

Be it pyramid scheme or MLM, the question is why are so many Americans drawn to these enterprises? In answer, greed, deception, economic insecurity, loss of community and pervasive commercialism in our culture all play their parts. These are the conventional explanations cited in newspaper reports when the illegal pyramid is prosecuted by local police or the investigative journalist documents once again that virtually no one makes a sustainable income in the MLM system.

However, a closer investigation reveals a more powerful force that is leading millions into the fraud and folly. With anecdote, testimony, research and logic, we will trace the motives for this mass phenomenon to a source that cannot be easily or glibly dismissed. The clear but, perhaps, discomforting answer to this question is that Amway, Nu Skin, NSA, Herbalife and the hundreds of other merchants of network marketing have converted so many of us into their itinerant sales reps because they appeal to treasured tenets of our faith.

Aimed right at the spiritual, community-minded nature of man, these companies are tapping into some of our most deeply held but least understood beliefs – beliefs that are so basic to American life that anyone who questions them is scorned as a heretic or as unpatriotic.

False Profits is a true story about some who lost faith in the prophets, profits and promises of pyramid schemes and multi-level marketing but gained profound knowledge of themselves. It is the honest recounting of extraordinary highs and antithetical lows – the excitement, the anticipation of success, the pain, the humiliation, the confusion, the self-challenge – that resulted from questing for financial and spiritual deliverance in the world of pyramid schemes and MLM.

In this retelling, there is a good deal of information about what some call today's most promising industry – MLM – and substantial evidence that can lead to the understanding of the term 'false profits' as it is applied to this industry. It will also become apparent that, in order to understand the beguiling appeal, the offered values and the allegedly spiritual messages of the MLM industry and pyramid schemes, we must look inward. After all, no one was ever forced to join an MLM organization or to enroll in a pyramid scheme.

Far from an exposé of an alien or negative force in our midst, *False Profits* offers an introspective examination of our own needs and beliefs. In the plot of this story, fraud and faith, myth and mysticism are seen to be closely linked as the specter of failure looks on.

The objective herein is not to save anyone from failing. It is, rather, to offer full disclosure about this system, the type of which would be given to any prospective investor as a precursor to participation in a franchise or security. The aim is to encourage people to look beyond government regulation of MLM in order to understand this industry's economic realities.

Neither a dream buster, *False Profits* invites you to determine, examine or reaffirm your highest ideals for a life that is worth living as it points out the profound distinctions between an existence founded upon material success as portrayed in the MLM solicitation and one that is dedicated to communal and spiritual vision. As part of this rocky but worthwhile and upward climb towards greater spirituality, we herein have the opportunity to share the renewed possibility of finding our authentic selves through a deeper, more satisfying and untainted spirituality.

Finally, *False Profits* serves to underscore the truth about our dreams, that they are woven out of our unique and infinitely complex gene structures and definitive personal experiences. In the writing, we have come to the sure knowledge that dreams are not about having but about living. And, most importantly, that dreams which are mass marketed – rather than privately nurtured in the soul – soon evaporate. True dreams are lived and expressed every day because they are the materializations of spiritual expression, the representations of our very beings. As it has served the authors so well in the writing, we offer the following content in the hope that it will provide the same useful purpose for others in the reading.

Section I
The Era of MLM

MLM: The New American Dream?

America, the home of the free and the brave, the land of opportunity, the place where all one's dreams can come true. It is, historically, the country where the poor and the dispossessed of the world have come to build a secure and promising future for themselves and their children. Over the years, the fulfillment of America's promise required commitment, persistence and sheer hard work. But the rewards for millions were real. History was our guarantor.

Today, America might seem a country where the old work ethics, standards and ideals have been replaced by a new paradigm. The current message seems to be that if you work smart, not hard, you can quickly and almost effortlessly become phenomenally wealthy. All you have to do is enroll in the latest multi-level marketing company or manipulate yourself into the right position in the newest pyramid scheme.

Prosperity comes not from your own labor but from the work of those below you on a distribution chain which feeds override commissions upward. Success requires not persistence but duplication. Hard work and long hours are obsolete. The only condition to making this system work is that you believe the doctrine and then convince others to believe in it, too. Attitude, faith, a demeanor of confidence and a conviction that extraordinary wealth is your destiny – these seem to be the keys to success and happiness in the 90's.

Where, you might ask, did this profound and fundamental shift begin to take place? When did pursuit of the American Dream slip from effort to enrollment, thereby tearing down the traditional wall separating the commercial from the communal? When and why did friends and family become prospects? In answer, we shall examine this process in its most flamboyant manifestations – multi-level marketing and associated illegal pyramid schemes.

In recent years, multi-level marketing – or MLM as it is known – has crept into the very heart of the business community, touching the lives of virtually all American consumers in one manner or another. The total MLM industry is now estimated to include between five and ten million distributors in America who sell some $10- to $20-billion of goods, mostly to each other. The larger of these operations have already reached their saturation points in the U.S.A. and are now concentrating on Asia and Latin America. In fact, this industry which was once concentrated in the aspiring lower and middle classes is now also penetrating the ranks of medical doctors, chiropractors, dentists and other high income professions.

Who has not been solicited? Who has not tried it? Who can even keep count of the times they have heard the utterance of telltale words – 'incredible opportunity,' 'momentum,' 'unlimited,' 'wealth beyond your imagination' – from family, friends and strangers alike all of whom show a sudden and inordinate interest in our very well-being as it relates to their new downline. Everyone has become a prospect.

The great majority of new distributors drop out of the system within a year only to be replaced by a new set of hopefuls, making the total number of Americans touched by MLM almost universal. That being the case and since MLM must insinuate itself into the fabric of family and community in order to grow, its influence on social and private life is immense. Yet, to date, it has remained essentially unexamined.

MLMs and pyramids are structurally the same, both relying upon an ever expanding chain of enrollment. The crucial and only difference is that pyramids amass their funds from enrollment fees while the MLM, to be legal, must engage in retail sales of some type of product or service. In a pyramid, the top levels are fueled only by recruitment of an ever-expanding base of hopefuls. There is no sustainable enterprise occurring other than paid enrollments. Mathematically, the very structure of MLMs or illegal pyramids disallows them from expanding indefinitely. If growth continues according to plan, later recruits will inevitably lose their financial investments. Those who launch pyramids know the ruinous course these programs will follow yet effectively dupe others into enrolling. Therefore, early entrants win at the calculated loss of the later enrollees.

Even though the largest of all MLMs, Amway, has reached a pinnacle in the American free enterprise system and despite the MLM recruitment rallies that offer the fulfillment of patriotic notions such as personal freedom and individual achievement, we will see that MLM is a false standard bearer of the American economic system.

Antithetical to the American spirit, the value system implicit in MLM measures achievement only in dollars. It belittles pursuits which do not amass great personal wealth. It limits our work opportunity, demeans our individuality and distorts the pursuit of happiness. In the end, acceptance of MLM's core values, even briefly or unconsciously, can account for the sense of humiliation and bewilderment experienced by so many who have churned through such programs.

The vast majority of America's opportunities do not promise and will never produce $50,000-a-month incomes. Rather, their value will be accounted for in as many other ways as there are people. For America's uniqueness is not in the number of its millionaires but in the extraordinary freedom offered to each of us to develop and express our individuality and cultivate our special talents and interests. These opportunities include unlimited options spanning art, entertainment, industry, academia, the professions, public service and virtually every entrepreneurial endeavor imaginable. America is truly a nation where the metaphysical maxim – if it can be imagined, it can be manifested – is demonstrated daily. And, it is faith in this type of opportunity that must be protected.

Since the beginning of this investigation into multi-level marketing and illegal pyramids, the mini-dramas of artful and deceptive enrollment practices in the MLM industry and raw examples of their damage to family and personal life have surfaced. Old friends send chain letter solicitations. Family members and neighbors become obsessive, addicted enrollees in Amway or NSA, another of the most prominent MLMs. Others confide strange encounters with what they describe as a cultish underworld trying to convert them to a new economy which promises extraordinary and easily-gained wealth.

Some former MLMers must actually seek outside help in breaking what they describe as a personal addiction to the promises of MLM. Others send out heart-rending requests for counsel for loved ones or close associates who appear to be lost in the MLM subculture, those who have become so deluded with dreams of becoming instant millionaires that they forsake or reject all contacts unless enrollment and sales might result. Clearly, far from becoming the new American Dream, MLM has in many instances become a national and recurring nightmare.

Spiritual Seekers - MLM's Chosen Ones

Multi-level marketing and illegal pyramid schemes are recent mass phenomena involving millions of people who come to these enterprises with a multitude of motivations, backgrounds and beliefs. Curiously – or not so curiously, as we shall see – a concentration of interest in MLM and illegal pyramids has been generated in the spiritual community and from that significant societal segment which has been loosely referred to as New

Age. Here is where our primary inquiry shall be focused.

New Age is among the newest of all forms of community representing millions of people who are joined globally, not by blood, flag, geography, history or founding father but by values and beliefs alone. The term New Age may seem indefinable or even presumptuous but there is a philosophical, sociological and psychological identity attached to it that undeniably unifies and energizes millions of people. In evidence, there are emerging psychographic[3] studies which are beginning to put clear definition to this population subset. Currently, there are other interesting indicators of shared preferences among those who would be identified as New Age thinkers, for example:

• Women in Los Angeles with household incomes of over $40,000 are more likely to have been to a channeler than to a psychiatrist, counselor or psychotherapist.

• 67% of Americans report having experienced E.S.P.

• 25% of Americans believe in reincarnation.

• More than $300 million worth of audio and video tapes demonstrating ways to harness mind power are sold annually.

• Shirley MacLaine's *Inner Workout* meditation video sold 100,000 copies in its first four months.

• Natural food is the fastest growing segment of the $300 billion retail food industry. [4]

---

[3] Psychographics is the study of markets based on people's attitudes and lifestyles which are increasingly being recognized as more influential on behavior, especially buying behavior, than traditional identifies of age and education, for example.

[4] Gathered by television producer, Diane Collins of Miami Beach, Florida, in a proposal for a television series on the New Age. Credits respectively: *L.A. Times;* University of Chicago; *US News and World Report; Forbes; Forbes; US News & World Report.*

Even with these types of shared characteristics, this community seems to defy strict definition. However, one central and defining tenet of this community – belief in the power of thought to change and create reality – is not ridiculed. In fact, the validity of this psychological or metaphysical concept is being accepted and incorporated into modern medical practice, sales training, professional sports, career planning, even into popular entertainment.

A long, illustrative list of examples could be assembled of recent movies and books that utilize the theme of metaphysical powers of thought and belief. *The Karate Kid* and its sequels, for instance, show a Zen master teaching an American youth the authority of and belief in creative visualization which results in the student's newfound ability to master karate and defeat competitors who have trained for many more years in the art. Indeed, the metaphysical miracles portrayed on the screen or in writing are coming to be seen as literally true and within the realm of experience of average Americans.

In his bestseller, *Megatrends 2000*, published at the beginning of the 90's decade, John Naisbitt estimated that there were approximately 20 million New Agers in the U.S., roughly 10% of the entire population of America. In some sections of the country such as in East and West Coast cities, Naisbitt estimated that the percentage may be as high as 12-15%. He wrote of these New Age people that they are "the most affluent, well-educated, successful segment of the baby boom." He quoted a representative of SRI's Values and Lifestyles Program who asserted that the influence of New Agers on the culture extends well beyond their number and further stated that "...they tend to set the trends."

The proposition that the growth of pyramid schemes and their legal MLM counterparts is driven by their unique appeal to a special strain of American faith which links and often equates riches with redemption is vividly documented in the dramatic events and commentary that follow. By looking at the MLM and pyramid scheme phenomena through the spectrum of New Age values and beliefs, we shall see in sharper resolution the propelling connections between belief and behavior.

The Religion of Abundance

History shows that the New Age movement and its 19th century predecessor, New Thought, have played unique roles in the sociological and philosophical development of modern America. Consequently, the New Age community is now the bearer of enormously powerful ideas which some historians believe have not only preserved the American belief in unlimited opportunity for every individual but now help to shape American business thinking.

Building on both the Puritan faith and the Protestant work ethic which linked virtue with labor, this emerging philosophy expanded to incorporate the Transcendentalism of Emerson and Thoreau, both champions of individuality and self-reliance who asserted an inspiring metaphysical connection between spirit and matter. This maturing belief system became codified, organized and widely disseminated in the New Thought religious congregations such as Christian Science, Unity and Science of Mind. More recently, it has connected with self-help and human potential courses by insinuating a direct relationship between financial abundance and spiritual enlightenment.

The first reference to success as the gaining of wealth appeared in an American dictionary only as recently as 1891. Prior to this date, success meant many other things. Two hundred years before success had been redefined in the popular mind as the gaining of wealth, the achievement that most Americans strived for was always in the context of a larger framework of values. Indeed, Puritan theology required that financial success be deeply connected to the common good. Seeking wealth was a public not private duty which was linked to virtue and its rewards were to be experienced as part of the broader good of the world not simply in the private accumulation of money. As sociologist Christopher

Lasch put it, the 19th century preached compulsive enterprise. But industry, thrift and temperance were promoted not merely as stepping stones to success but rather as their own rewards. Even the most unabashed exponents of self-enrichment clung to the notion that wealth derived value from its contribution to the general good and to the happiness of future generations.[5]

As the importance of these traditional values declined, wealth by itself became the sign of God's blessing upon the righteous. Lack of wealth was the sign of alienation from the Universal First Cause. Historian Richard Weiss noted the seamless connection between New Thought's tenets of faith and earlier orthodox Protestantism in which the power to believe and then manifest reality from belief was a modern form of placing your trust in God or having faith in the Divine. The subconscious, Weiss and others observed, later became the link to the Divine replacing prayer or even the intervention of saints. Thus, by conditioning the subconscious, one could connect directly to the Universal Being.

In the new creed, wealth manifests by simply thinking continuously and affirmatively about it. Such affirmations are the means by which one can spiritually align with the higher order. The advanced thought is that lack of wealth is not prescribed or intended for anyone but is only the result of one's failing to align with the Universal Will. As such, each individual is personally and totally responsible for his or her own destiny and the means to attain prosperity are available to all in light of intention, will and faith.

The great contribution of New Age precursor, New Thought, was to replenish America's faith in opportunity and personal entrepreneurship in

---

5 Christopher Lasch, *The Culture of Narcissism: American Life in an Age of Diminishing Expectations.* New York: W. W. Norton & Co., 1978, page 57.

response to seeming and increasing personal powerlessness in the face of huge financial organizations. New Thought asserted – and New Age currently attempts to prove – that the power to rise in the world financially depends not on current economic conditions but only on one's personal mental attitude. Therefore, not only are frugality and hard work unnecessary, they are irrelevant to the outcome. Wealth can be achieved painlessly and inevitably by simply aligning with Universal Intelligence which wills us all to be healthy and prosperous.

The American tradition of Puritanism that had undergirded free enterprise and the wealth-seeking way of life was, thus, superseded by a new religion which took up this very same banner of seeing financial achievement as a sign of God's beneficence. Even as science and plundering corporations eroded the values governing the quest for wealth, New Thought – then New Age – restored America's faith in the individual and offered its own sets of rationalizations and credos.

The full embrace of the metaphysics of prosperity consciousness by the mainstream culture can be reliably dated to the mid-1980's during a time when taxes were reduced and the debt ceiling was all but eliminated. In words and demeanor, then-President Reagan represented boundless optimism and faith in America's destiny of global economic dominance and moral leadership. Communism and all its lesser varieties of collectivist and social engineering policies were literally being called evil. Greed became good as the stock market rose Prometheus-like. The anxieties and cynicism of the post-Vietnam and post-Watergate eras were being shed. Supply-side economics was in vogue and trickle-down prosperity for the masses was confidently predicted.

High interest rates, inflation, the skyrocketing federal deficit, rising personal debt, credit card abuse, the decline of American manufacturing, the dangers of staking so much on the abstractions of financial futures, the growing disparity between the haves and the have-nots and other such domestic indicators all receded in importance. The larger picture representing economic growth and expansion held our attention. Faith and confidence were deemed the only essential factors to a future of success.

Prosperity consciousness was being fully embraced by Dale Carnegie and a host of other business boosters, sales trainers, motivators and speakers who applied the philosophy to business and taught it as a new technique for personal advancement and competitive advantage. The original and transforming philosophy of the New Age movement was, thus, becoming indistinguishable from the values and promises of the acquisitive consumer society. True to its self-definition as societal explorer and harbinger, the New Age movement anticipated and set the trend, then helped lead America into a new way of thinking about labor and wealth and their relationship to spirituality.

It seems from the history of the New Age movement that one precept – called prosperity consciousness – has been singled out and is enjoying extraordinary power in America today. Historically, its roots are traceable to the Puritan work ethic but, over the last century and a half, the concept of prosperity consciousness has undergone a major transformation. Prosperity, originally a transcendent state of being, has become defined as simply financial wealth and has been stripped of any of traditional Puritan values of community responsibility or personal standards of behavior. All the cosmological and spiritual authority it originally carried has been transferred directly to the business of accumulating wealth. Therefore, over time, success has come to mean only one thing – financial achievement.

Without balancing spiritual and social values, these ideas can feed the insatiable American appetite for commercial growth and expansion as they justify personal avarice. Indeed, they can serve as triggers and motivators for rapacious and irresponsible activity. The Airplane Game pyramid scam that swept through the New Age community in the late 1980's and which is dramatically recounted in upcoming pages is a quintessential example of how a good idea, lacking any countervailing values and taken to its logical conclusion, turns to madness.

Prosperity in the Modern Day

The story picks up in the latter years of the decade just months before the stock market crash of 1987. Even as it shattered some paper futures, this event did not shake the national faith in Wall Street's destiny to provide God-given and unending prosperity. Nowhere was this faith in abundance and prosperity held more intently than in the New Age community, stronghold of the chosen people in the chosen land. It was at this point that the merger of mainstream American thinking and New Age philosophy would result in the acceptance of MLM into the traditional business world.

After languishing on the fringe since the late 1950's as largely shunned and discredited, the multi-level marketing movement catapulted into economic expansion in the late 1980's. This was not mere coincidence but, rather, inevitable given the potent beliefs of the New Age as they were adopted by an economy dependent upon faith and optimism. MLM was simply positioned to take its place in the ranks of legitimate business as an industry whose driving force and true products are hopes and promises, leaving faith and finance clearly indivisible.

At this point, it is worth noting that while the New Age is the primary focus of this work, it is not to suggest that people who identify with the ideas and values of New Age are the main constituents or proponents of MLM or pyramid schemes. To the contrary, MLM and many of the blatantly illegal pyramids adapt, chameleon-like, to numerous segments of the larger community. Yet in all these various formats, MLM and all pyramid schemes rely upon the core belief which is so elementally revealed in the New Age community. In this modern American Dream, wealth comes not from frugality, hard work or ingenuity but from being at the right place at the right time. And, faith will take you to this mythic and magical place.

No surprise then that there are countless examples of MLM creeping into the most sacred of places. Witness evangelist Pat Robertson who started his own MLM company and enrolled thousands of his congregation by proclaiming it a form of "prosperity theology." Or motivator and evangelist Robert Schuller who sells his tape program through MLM organizations and calls it Positive Thinking. In 1988, thousands of middle class African-Americans were caught up in a swindle which played upon America's faith in an ever-expanding economy. Dubbed the Corporate Ladder, *Black Enterprise* Magazine wrote that it was "the rage in black communities from Brooklyn to southwest Los Angeles." So it is that we can see pyramid schemes and MLMs flourishing among such diverse factions as Fundamentalist Christian churches and specifically targeted professions such as physicians, dentists and chiropractors.

According to today's most popular MLM promotional book, *Wave 3: The New Era in Network Marketing* by Richard Poe, the 1980's actually marked the second wave of development for MLM with an explosion in the number of companies and distributors. Still showing robust growth and profitability in the 1990's, MLM has continued its expansion with some companies selling shares on the major stock exchanges although many business journalists and analysts remain leary of their longer term investment worth. Oddly, a major contributor to this extraordinary growth was the federal court decision which declared the Amway Corporation, the largest of all MLMs, a legal business after the Federal Trade Commission lost its case of trying to prove that Amway was founded on a pyramid scheme.

As we will soon see, it was the social philosophy of New Age in its most recent metamorphosis that served as the bold rationale for the Airplane Game scheme, the Fund America fraud and other such follies. Similarly in the legalized multi-level marketing industry, this philosophy plays a central and defining role for enrolling and inspiring distributors. Faith in a destiny of prosperity is proclaimed as the main requirement for quick and certain wealth. Thus we can easily see that the study of the MLM and pyramid scheme phenomena through the experience of the New Age community is, prophetically, a study of mainstream America.

The MLM Catechism

Wherever there is a faith there must be a catechism which is to be studied, recited and taught by its followers. The MLM industry which is in the business of selling faith makes far greater use of the catechism of the New Age than any other business sector in the American economy. Through books, audio tapes, videos, recruitment rallies and millions of personal training sessions, this new American business philosophy – promising wealth to those with vision and belief – is aggressively propagated. Similarly, as the economics of pyramids require unceasing expansion at exponential rates, its catechism must be spread at an even more intense pace. In other words, many more will be called than will follow.

Unlike those of traditional sales training or conventional business and finance, MLM's lessons are infused with a sense of the divine. The principles that undergird its foundation are advanced not just as laws of economics but as the laws of the Universe which can be plainly seen in one genre title, *God Wants You to Be Rich*.[6] Found in this book's chapters are not just mundane economic principles, rather, we encounter the "theology of economics." Libraries file this book and others of its ilk in two sections, Economics and Economics-Religious. As it is no less than a manifesto of a financial religion, it would seem appropriate to view this as another catechism rather than as a book on simple business boosterism.

In these more modern faiths, the assertion is that God explicitly desires personal wealth for the faithful. Poverty is no mere misfortune and certainly not a virtue for which one is blessed. In fact, poverty is viewed as no less than a sin. The thinking follows

---

[6] Paul Zane Pilzer, *God Wants You to Be Rich: The Theology of Economics*. New York: Simon & Schuster, 1995.

that the means to attain this abundant state of grace and achieve its attendant wealth involve spiritual and psychological choice.

The way in which America came into possession of this new type of faith can be more clearly understood through a study of the Christian Science, Mind Cure and faith healing movements and similar veins of thought which linked spirit and matter. In fact, it was the quest for spiritual healing of the body that led to what is known today as prosperity consciousness or, as some Christian evangelists refer to it, prosperity theology.

During the 19th century, metaphysics – a belief in a higher reality which governs and explains physical behavior – had enabled Christians to maintain their divine connectedness with God despite the findings of science which linked man to lower animals. Through affirmations, religious ceremonies and prayer, Christian Science and its offshoot groups 'proved' the existence of a higher plane, a natural philosophy that governed physical science.[7] Consequently, faith healings were called scientific demonstrations of a higher metaphysical reality.

While Christian Scientists viewed the use of these principles to gain money as a distortion and a manipulation, others logically deduced that metaphysical applications should be able to produce financial as well as physical health. The power resided in alignment with the Universal Will. This power, at least potentially, was available to everyone

---

[7] Mark Twain believed that Christian Science would eventually sweep the entire country and become the prevailing religion, such was its power and momentum in later years of the 19th century. From extensive personal investigation, Twain concluded that Christian Science unquestionably delivered on its promise of healing through metaphysical treatments. Did it also result in the needless deaths of some members due to lack of conventional medical care? Yes, Twain decided, but it probably killed no more people than did traditional medicine. Mark Twain, *Christian Science*. New York: Harper & Brothers, 1902.

and in all endeavors of life. Eventually, it became creed that if God wanted us to be physically healthy, surely He also desired our financial health.

Any investigation into the history of the New Age will quickly reveal what may seem, at first, an odd connection between health and wealth. Yet, these two seemingly distant fields of medicine and economics are now philosophically bound together. Today's New Age bookstores are replete with therapies, diets and lifestyle regimens focused on achieving a longer and healthier life. Found in the same section are the metaphysical remedies for overcoming poverty and achieving wealth and leisure.

Some historians date the shift from New Thought's obsession with spiritual healing to using its technique for gaining wealth with the publication in 1897 of Ralph Waldo Trine's *In Tune With the Infinite* [8] which became one of the greatest non-fiction bestsellers of the 20th century. From this point forward, the spiritual concepts associated with New Thought have been as concerned with conjuring up wealth as with sustaining health.

---

[8] Though this book has been cited as a turning point in the direction and focus of New Thought, a reading of the book shows the reticence of New Thought teachers to convert their philosophy into a technology for making money. This task awaited business writers several generations later. Trine did state that "the old idea of godliness as poverty has absolutely no basis for its existence, and the sooner we get away from it the better....Faith, absolute dogmatic faith is the only law of true success." However, in his chapter entitled, "Plenty of All Things – The Law of Prosperity," he also stated, "He who is enslaved with the sole desire for material possessions here will continue to be enslaved even after he can no longer retain his body... The one who has come into the realization of the higher life no longer has a desire for the accumulation of enormous wealth... Many a person is living in a palace today who in the real life is poorer than many a one who has not even a roof to cover him." Trine referred to the obsessive materialism as a "loathsome disease of the body" and a "species of insanity."

The most recent illustration of the philosophical connections between health and wealth can be found in the recently popularized career of Deepak Chopra. His early metaphysical books were focused on creating good health, e.g. *Perfect Health, Quantum Healing, Creating Health* and his blockbuster, *Ageless Body, Timeless Mind.* However, Chopra then followed the now well-traveled path leading from creating health to creating wealth as can be seen in his subsequent offerings, *Creating Affluence* and *The Seven Spiritual Laws of Success.*[9]

While formerly rooted in Puritan theology and Calvinism, success in America has been largely viewed as cosmological. This shift began to take place in the post-Protestant era when the laws of metaphysics began to replace the traditional Protestant work ethic as the philosophical support structure for entrepreneurship. In fact, New Thought or mind power disdained the Protestant values of frugality, economy and community obligation, instead proclaiming the new painless values of ease, relaxation and comfort. Thus, a way of thinking replaced a way of acting.

As historian Richard Weiss noted, "Using Emerson's Transcendentalism, mind power referred to God as the Universal Intelligence. Man is part of this divinity and, therefore, can think his way to success by aligning with cosmic force. Mind is equated with soul. A healthy mind is a healthy soul. Virtue is identified with health rather than frugality, prudence and industry. Sickness is sin and sickness is incompatible with success just as laziness was in an earlier era. This new approach stressed not virtue but psychological techniques of self-manipulation as a means to achievement. Mind power gave the

---

[9] Note another interesting overview of this metaphysical magician in "Deepak Chopra Has a Cold" by Chip Brown, *Esquire* magazine, October 1995, pp. 118-125.

individual his freedom. He only had to align with universal laws and all things were possible."[10]

It is this new American faith in prosperity shorn of any social consequences or qualifying personal values that fuels the MLM movement. It enables the movement to enroll thousands of new recruits in the face of 99% economic casualty rates. It also provides the modern rationalization and dream-like appeal which encourages honest, tax-paying Americans to join illegal pyramid schemes.

The publishing of these ideas and beliefs has today grown into a vast industry that is so intertwined with the MLM movement that it is difficult to separate the two. MLM uses the catechism to argue the historical inevitability of its selling methods and the cosmic truth of its cause. New Age publishers use MLM to market their books and tapes. MLM teaches the health/wealth catechism to its distributors and then sells them the New Age remedies, herbs, vitamins, weight-loss formulas, subliminal tapes and other inspirational media to re-train the subconscious.

More powerful than any product, charismatic leader or compensation plan, the literature of faith is the prime tool used to recruit and to persuade new distributors to join MLM sales organizations. Once enrolled in the system, the new distributors are urged to buy more of these materials on a weekly basis, making MLM distributors a prime market for these products.

Consider the circularity of this process. The MLM company provides the new recruit with the metaphysical literature of visualization, belief and the power to manifest a new reality of wealth and luxury. Inspired by this hopeful and appealing message, the convert joins the MLM company which presents itself as the necessary wealth-producing

---

[10] Richard Weiss, *The American Myth of Success from Horatio Alger to Norman Vincent Peale*. New York: Basic Books, 1969, p. 14.

vehicle. The transcendent plan for achieving the promised wealth calls for selling the inspiring literature to more recruits. As the message is spread in evangelistic fashion, the new recruit will reap the profits from on-going sales into infinity just as the literature prophesied. Believing it makes it happen.

This circular system has been most grandly and controversially employed by distributors of the Amway Corporation, the biggest of all MLMs. For instance, Amway's largest distributor, Dexter Yager of Charlotte, North Carolina, operates a $35 million-a-year business selling motivational and inspirational tapes to his downline distributors. Dream big. Be persistent and consistent. Avoid negative thinking, the tapes exhort the faithful. Each week, tens of thousands of Yager distributors pay five dollars or more for the featured audiocassette. The tape-of-the-week is shipped to 50 states and 10 foreign countries.

Yager and his supporters say the tapes and books help people succeed by bolstering their faith, the key to making dreams come true. "You've got to keep them dreaming," Yager advised in a fall, 1995 edition of *Dream Builders*, his network magazine. "Take them dreaming . . . so that they get hungry for the things they're not satisfied with, what they have won't do... We've got to keep them looking at houses, boats, planes, cars, vans, expanding and stimulating and fertilizing that powerful brain that God gave every one of them until they believe they deserve more and they will go after it and they will get it."

In a 1995 three-part analysis of the Dexter Yager empire, the *Charlotte Observer* noted that some Amway dropouts say "the endless stream of motivation aids keeps marginal salespeople believing – in the face of poor results – that success is just around the bend."

"The tapes and books kept me brainwashed," said one ex-distributor who was quoted in the series after having spent 13 years in Yager's Amway network. "They get you in this frame of mind that you need to feed on the materials in order to survive." He said the barrage of motivation aids put him "in a performance trap" where he obsessed about achieving but felt mired in failure. He had spent $30,000 on tapes, books and rallies before dropping out of Amway and filing bankruptcy in 1992.

A Pennsylvania lawsuit recently filed by former Amway distributors called the tape selling plan "a pyramid-type scheme" which has "coerced" thousands of Amway recruits into purchasing marginally useful materials. The terse language of the suit reads, "At all times relevant hereto, defendants Britt and Yager (Bill Britt and Dexter Yager, the largest Amway distributors in the world) regularly represented to plaintiffs that their success as Amway distributors was contingent upon the purchase of defendants Britt and Yager's motivational materials, and that without such materials plaintiffs would be unable to build and maintain successful Amway distributorships."

The plaintiffs alleged that <u>selling inspirational tapes to downline sales reps is a more profitable business to Amway's largest distributors than selling Amway products</u> themselves. Officially, they are treated by Amway as sales tools. But, in other MLM organizations, the inspirational material containing their catechisms has, indeed, risen beyond the status of marketing material to that of official product.

One of America's fastest growing MLMs, Nutrition for Life, which was founded by marketer Kevin Trudeau sells the inspirational cassette tapes of the largest publisher of New Age catechism materials, Nightingale-Conant, as one of its core products. In fact, a Nightingale-Conant Nutrition for Life on-line promotional message to new distributors informs them, "Now you can target your inner self with valuable resource programs. These self-improvement tools unlock the powers of the mind. You can commit to making a personal difference by equipping yourself to achieve your goals and attain the success you deserve."

What can result from using – and selling – these personal development cassettes that target the inner self? For this, the company turns to the inevitable pyramid mathematics of the multi-level marketing industry. Each one has a slightly different twist on the math but, essentially, all lead to the exponential growth potential.

"On the 7th level," the literature states, "the income potential for sponsoring just 8 (new distributors) personally goes to 18% per month or $294,912. With the 4x7 Forced Matrix Compensation Plan with spillover and a massive nationwide advertising campaign by marketing experts reaching millions with this opportunity, our success has great potential," the new recruit is informed.

In keeping with the New Age tradition of linking wealth-building with a healthy life, the other products of Nutrition for Life are vitamins and herbs. Identifying itself with the philosophical precepts of the New Age upon which all MLM enrollment campaigns are based, Nutrition for Life ends its advertisement with its trademark New Age aphorism, "Success Is the Natural State of the Universe."

Over the past fifty years, the metaphysical message that MLM relies upon so strongly – chiefly, that a person becomes what he thinks about – has permeated public thought in America. Clearly, the idea that a person can reinvent his personality, position in society and personal happiness by simply willing it has powerful democratic appeal.

In the 1990's, this idea has taken political form in the message that personal responsibility should be emphasized over social welfare concerns. The primary concentration for delivery of this message is in the motivation industry where it is most fervently taught and utilized in the area of business sales with the MLM industry taking a striking lead in the use of this selling strategy.

In a four part article entitled "Is There a Science of Success?" in the February, 1994 edition of *The*

Atlantic Monthly, writer Nicholas Lemann examined the assertions of prosperity thinking in light of academic research and how it manifests itself in American life.

Lemann observed that, for the most part, the predominant concepts of prosperity consciousness are contained in an audio tape by Earl Nightingale called "The Strangest Secret." The publisher of this tape, Nightingale-Conant, claims it has outsold any other audio tape in history. Lemann wondered why the idea of employing motivational and affirmative techniques to reshape the subconscious is dominated by business boosters and professional promoters rather than by social scientists in the academic fields of psychology or sociology.

It would seem, he noted, that an idea of such power and potential for helping people would be more seriously studied in universities. Instead, as he demonstrated, it is almost totally promulgated by audio tape publishers like Nightingale-Conant as a technology for making money. The motivation industry, as he termed it, is skewed toward fast-growing areas like Southern California, Florida and Texas and is aimed at salesmen and people who are ambitious but not comfortably settled into a role.

Lemann traced the career of David C. McClelland, a psychologist and former Harvard professor who now teaches at Boston University. In mainstream academia, Lemann said, Dr. McClelland has the most substantial record to date of examining the relationship between motivation and economic success. Among his former students were Timothy Leary and Richard Alpert, now better known as Baba Ram Dass.

The Atlantic Monthly article concluded that, despite more than 40 years of work, neither McClelland nor anyone else in the academic world has succeeded in establishing a strong or predictable link between the techniques of prosperity thinking and actual economic advancement or personal happiness. Nonetheless, there are barrages of claims that are put forth by sales trainers and self improvement course developers such as Life Spring and the Forum that would have followers believe otherwise. More importantly, the article acknowledged that the values that are associated with this thinking – greed, ambition, manipulation and narrow-minded self-promotion – have demeaned it as an area for serious inquiry.

David Winter, a researcher who has worked closely with Dr. McClelland and who has developed a technique for scoring political speeches and other texts for motivational content, was asked by Lemann to listen to "The Strangest Secret." Winter acknowledged the practical usefulness of some of the techniques offered but went on to say, "This stuff is largely enmeshed in a set of values... (in which) all goals come down to money."

The theme of Lemann's extensive article was to expose the potential importance of linking how we think or, more importantly, how we can change the way we think, to improving the fortunes and satisfactions of our lives. If motivation to succeed really was both measurable and teachable, Lemann asserted, it would have profound effects upon society. He concluded that the study of the subject deserved the respect and attention of academia, government and psychology. At the present time, however, and in light of the value system in which it largely operates, as he put it, "about the only place such discussion occurs is on infomercials."

A New Age-oriented reader of the *Atlantic* article might take exception to the placing of positive mental attitude, Nightingale's "Strangest Secret," motivational techniques, psychological testing and the spiritual concept of prosperity consciousness all in the same category. This same reader might also wonder how anyone could truly question whether reshaping our minds leads directly to reshaping our lives. To the New Ager, this is a self-evident reality.

But who can deny the conclusion that this fundamental belief has been usurped and dominated by the larger belief system of seeking happiness through wealth and consumption? What we now call prosperity consciousness began as a transcendent and spiritual concept which specifically avoided attaching purpose and objectives to prayer, relying instead upon trust in and alignment with a higher power.

Formulated and articulated originally by a small band of Transcendentalists who eschewed the commercialization of life, it has evolved into its present form as a financially-driven body of techniques. Moving from its status as a spiritual philosophy, it now lives as secret technology for success. This secret is bought and sold daily and is put forth as the foundation and justification for the most outrageous, hopeless and often illegal schemes. In fact, those who are today's self-appointed spiritual standard bearers of the original message have largely become indistinguishable from the business boosters and promoters of the motivation industry.

In the coming chapters we will look at what kinds of personal and communal realities are manifested by a spiritual philosophy in which "all goals come down to money."

Section II
The Scene of a Crime

False Profits

The Setup

*And so again I say: It is
shockingly right instead of
shockingly wrong for you to be
prosperous. Obviously, you
cannot be very happy if you are
poor and you need not be poor.
It is a sin.* [11]

— Catherine Ponder

We all gathered together that Sunday, appropriately, in a church. Yet, we were not genuflecting before the traditional altars to which our parents had in the past taken us. Jewish, Catholic, Protestant, we were all now united in the praising and celebration of the faith, New Age. Well-known spiritual leaders, husband and wife, had been invited to address us not in accord with any ecclesiastical calendar but in keeping with our minister's intuition of what we most wanted and needed in the moment.

On that day of worship, we were assembled to pray, to learn, to meditate and to be shown proven rituals for touching the face of God. We were not waiting for the next life to stand before the Creator. Actually, our speakers would be discussing a kind of technology for achieving the ultimate even as we proceeded to live in the imperfect present – the now. Well, not exactly now, but in the not too distant

---

[11] Catherine Ponder, *The Dynamic Laws of Prosperity.* DeVorss & Company, 1985, pp. 11-13. Ponder is one of the best known prosperity teachers of New Thought/New Age. In *The Dynamic Laws of Prosperity*, she comments "Please note that the word 'rich' means having an abundance of good or living a fuller, more satisfying life. Indeed, you are prosperous to the degree that you are experiencing peace, health, happiness and plenty in our world." Yet, Ms. Ponder herself contributed mightily to a distortion of this philosophy with her ample use of the term millionaire in her book titles and speeches.

future. The deficiency of our now was, of course, the reason we were gathered. We were deeply dissatisfied with our present condition. It was not onerous. It simply was not enough.

How odd since not one of us could have been called poverty-stricken by the living standards of America. By worldwide measures, we were, in fact, among the luckiest human beings on the planet. We all drove to our gathering in nice cars. We all had homes and were well-fed. We were literate, educated and, for the most part, well-traveled. We had televisions, CD players and in-vogue wardrobes. We all ate regularly in restaurants, took vacations, had telephones, fax machines and computers.

Yet, spiritually, we had defined ourselves as impoverished. Whatever level of affluence we had attained was clearly not enough. Our constant worries, debts, insecurities and unfulfilled desires were the overwhelming evidence of our lack. Redemption, we reasoned, must, therefore, lie in deliverance to a new level of affluence. Like the Virgin Mary, it beckoned to us with outstretched arms urging us to "Come, come, my children. I am the way to Your Lord and Savior." The Madonna of prosperity seemed beautiful, gracious and kind. This day, as New Age supplicants, we had gathered to bask in her light and to learn the means by which we could create and manifest it in our lives and bank accounts.

Not a part of the teachings of our youth, none of us could explain how we had all come to this mutually held belief as to what would make us whole and complete. Yet this very belief was the central tenet of our congregation and it was the reason our leader had, with such confidence, known that the day's speakers would be eagerly welcomed. In demand not only for our group but for similar New Age church groups all over America, they preach a methodology for salvation. As it is a joyous and optimistic message, our leader knew that we would feel wonderful upon hearing it and would contribute generously to the church after receiving it.

Our middle-aged spiritual guides were amusing yet profound. How well they seemed to know us, to appreciate our weaknesses, our follies, our obsessions. Without offending, they acknowledged the failures that we held ourselves to be. They knew because they, too, had once been there. Yet, in their new life they exuded success. Their clothes were bold and stylish, worn with obvious comfort and ease. The husband of the couple sported a gold earring and made reference to lovingly exchanged gifts of expensive jewelry. They told of their Grand Seville Cadillac and their many vacations to exotic resorts. They had obviously arrived at the place we all longed to be.

They had not come to castigate, criticize or gloat. Their message was one of hope and optimism. Their focus was on what we could manifest, on our potential, our creativity. We were reminded that the Universe, God, the Great Spirit, whatever we wanted to call it, wants us to be wealthy. With the ultimate cosmic cause on our side, how could we fail? Well, only by rejecting or ignoring the benevolent influence. With enlightenment, with good intention, excellent results were inevitable. Our lives would change dramatically and inexorably for the better.

We were assured that the entire will of the Universe was focused upon each and every one of us. "Stand in that white light," they advised us. "Feel its saving and healing energy." We were reminded that universal prosperity begins with each of us, that our personal affluence would be the most powerful contribution we could make toward ending the misery that oppresses the world. God would not allow such misery without a good reason.

This was called prosperity. And, yes, prosperity could certainly lift the heavy burdens of worry, work-related stress, low self-esteem, family dysfunction, even eating disorders. Its achievement could confirm to us and the rest of the world that we were in alignment with the universal principles of benevolence as surely as poverty is a sign of discord and resistance. You see, the Universe wants us to be prosperous. Suddenly we were clear that those who are not affluent have brought this condition upon themselves

Prosperity was not defined in great detail, yet most of us seemed to envision it in annual figures of six or more – roughly double or better than what most of us had ever earned. For some, it may have been a million and for others it may have been exactly the very income that some were already earning yet had found to be completely insufficient. Whatever the amount, it was beyond our immediate reach yet not so far away that we could not envisage it. Our pulses raced at the mere thought. We realized that the exact personal pathway to prosperity was vague but attainable. Further, we could achieve it without struggle, more education, starting a new career or working more hours. Happily, even the mere thought of cutting back on our cash-driven lifestyles had been erased.

We were told that gaining prosperity does not involve special study of the means by which to attain it or close examination of business decisions or investments. Far more deserving of our attention was an analysis of and a shift in our way of thinking. For it was our thinking and only our thinking that stood between us and a quantum leap in personal development. Prosperity, we were taught, begins with a new consciousness, akin to a state of grace. Prosperous people are not known by their actions but by their attitudes. And while we may not have control over inflation, unemployment, our cultural or economic backgrounds or the state of the local marketplace, we certainly have total power over our thinking and our attitudes. The keys to prosperity are, therefore, completely within our hands. We have only to learn how to use them. Extraordinary wealth and luxury are just that close.

Buoyed by a message of happiness that assured a future of wealth, we were ready to take the steps that would align us with this destiny which would begin to unfold, we were told, as we commenced to give. One must only choose a spiritual source of prosperity, give to it generously and it will return to you ten-fold. This formula, we were informed, is based upon the universal and immutable principle of tithing. Giving is no longer unconditional, based upon love or even upon the needs of those to whom we give. Now it is offered as a prescription for actually returning ten dollars for each one we donate. In this new mode of thinking, giving is actually based upon our own needs rather than on those of the recipients of our generosity.

One more element of the prescription is necessary to produce the beneficent results. It is that we must be clear about what we want in return. If it is a Mercedes, we must visualize that beautiful, new, shining car. We must put pictures of it in our house. We must know its color. We must be able to smell that leather interior. The immutable laws of prosperity consciousness require crystal clarity of goals and intentions.[12]

As a meditation, we closed our eyes and vividly imagined ourselves with the items of our desires. We sighed and smiled while sensuously relishing the images of luxurious and effortless lives. Some of us shed tears in realization of how we had been depriving ourselves by harboring beliefs in scarcity or nursing the spiritual afflictions of shame or guilt.

We could now confidently harness the will of the Universe with our minds and tactically tithe to our church – or spiritual leaders – and, thus, be led to our heaven on earth very soon...

Close your eyes and relax. Let the cool darkness of the room and the soothing music bring you to your

---

[12] Life goals chosen by those at religious gatherings where prosperity consciousness is taught are inevitably the same goals that electrify MLM and pyramid scheme meetings. We see churches bless and sanctify these goals without remark despite their acquisitive nature promising 10-to-1 returns through the immutable laws of tithing which is an improvement over the 8-to-1 returns promised in, for example, the Prosperity Game.

center. As you go within, realize the timelessness of the moment. There is no beginning, no end. Just this moment.

Starting with your toes, stretch, then relax. Release the tension in your feet, your ankles. Focus on your calves and allow the stress to drain from them. Unbend your knees and feel the ease extending into your thighs. Now become conscious of your genitals and notice how pleasurable they feel. Know that pleasure is your natural state.

Breathe slowly and deeply and permit any tension to recede from your intestines and lower abdomen. No more straining and controlling. You are now letting Nature and God overtake you. Know that the most powerful form of energy takes no effort at all.

Feel your chest open and your shoulders lower. You do not need to hold them tightly as if to protect your heart. You can open up now. Next let the wrinkles unfurrow, the frown disappear from your forehead. Let your mouth and lips come to rest in a blissful expression of acceptance. This is the smile of God, the God that is within all of us.

You have struggled. You have worried. You have worked so hard. All of that is over now. You have arrived. The path has been long but you know it is the right path because the Universe does not make mistakes. There are no accidents. Everything is for a purpose.

What lies ahead is love and comfort and freedom. The illusions of limitation and scarcity have been lifted. The pain that you needed to go through is complete. Imagine now that you can have whatever you want and go wherever you wish to go. Allow your mind to focus on the things and places you have longed to possess or experience. This is your God-vision. And it is yours to claim. There is no scarcity. There is plenty for all. God did not create an insufficient world.

Life, as you know, is a perfect projection of our inner thoughts, our collective unconscious manifesting itself as what we commonly, however mistakenly, call reality. Thus, we create reality, day by day, minute by minute.

When we think love and prosperity, we shall create it. But it takes more than just thought. It requires aligning with the Universal Will as well. When the Universe beckons, as it does now, we must answer. It is not action that is needed but an end to resistance. You have been resisting. Now you can enter the stream, go with the flow of life and receive the abundance. Simply be willing to name your bliss.

A regal black Mercedes with luxurious leather upholstery... a sleek red sports car... a stylish and comfortable home magnificently appointed and overlooking the ocean or a spectacular valley... all the luxuries... satin sheets, pearls, gold and diamonds... fragrant, sensuous perfumes... fine restaurants, vintage wines... and cash, lots and lots of beautiful green cash, piled high or strewn carelessly everywhere you look.

Picture it all. Taste it. Smell it. Feel it. Fondle it. For it is yours now, just as God intended. Prosperity and abundance are the natural gifts of life when perfect alignment is attained. I promise you this.

Now say, yes... Yes... YES... OH, YEESSS!

The Outlaw Network

So it was that we, freely and joyously, stepped onto the New Age pathway joining countless others who were also earnestly seeking enlightenment. The journey began with the embracing of a dogmatic yet revered metaphysical prophecy of abundance which encompassed a vision of both financial wealth and spiritual deliverance.

Our Hondas, high-end Toyotas, Saabs and Volvos occupied every available guest space in the condominium complex. We were all gathered together again – at least 75 familiar faces – warmly and comfortably crowded into the living room, dining room and kitchen then spilling out onto the patio, all eager to hear the speaker standing on the stairway. Safely among friends and colleagues, enveloped by consensus and congeniality, our usual skeptical defenses had been left at home. On that brisk February evening in South Florida, we were all ready to expand our horizons, to grasp new possibilities and to deepen our connectedness.

Over the previous 10 years or so, most of us who gathered that evening had participated in various human potential and New Age courses and seminars. Many of us had done the est training and its follow-up advanced seminars. Some were graduates of Life Spring or other variations such as the Loving Relationship Training (LRT) and the Insight Course. Some belonged to Unity Church or the Church of Religious Science. We frequented New Age book stores and health food stores, read Shirley MacLaine, Napoleon Hill and Wayne Dyer and listened to the healing, meditative tapes of Louise Hay and Bernie Siegel. Many of us had had our astrological charts done, witnessed channelings, gone through a re-birthing process, regularly enjoyed massage therapy and accepted the idea of a past life even while not particularly planning for our next one. Many had tried acupuncture for various ailments, taken vitamins and herbs, drunk herbal teas, avoided red meat, owned at least one crystal and meditated, at least, on occasion. Yoga rather than jogging was the exercise of choice for many who were gathered that evening.

Although we may not have known one another's last names or even first names without the benefit of name tags, a modern kind of intimacy bound us together. In group encounters and in breakthrough seminars, most of us had been lamenting our hopes, examining our illusions, marveling at the patterns of our lives. We had shared our broken marriages, estranged relationships with parents or children along with the elusive sense of emptiness that plagued our work lives. We revealed our sexual secrets and found them to be so commonplace as to be laughable even as we retrieved them, reinstating our shame. In every course we took, we learned again that our lives are only what we make them. As to objectivity or reality – all an illusion. Life is what we declare it to be in our silent, inner conversations. Change the content of the conversation and the objective world miraculously transforms. We, of course, change with it. Abundance and prosperity are always available if only we will allow them to enter our lives. The Universe works perfectly. It is only we who are discordant.

Most of us assembled that evening were 25- to 50-year old, college-educated Caucasians from middle class backgrounds who were managerial or professional by occupation. Interspersed among us were some from the gay community, a few from other races. Without ever having counted, it seemed that a large percentage of us had been raised Jewish or Catholic, so we shared many common values and ethical standards.

We were establishing a network, that much heralded institution discussed in *Megatrends*[13] by

---

[13] John Naisbitt, *Megatrends, Ten New Directions Transforming Our Lives*. New York: Warner Books, 1982.

John Naisbitt and Marilyn Ferguson's *Aquarian Conspiracy*.[14] Certainly, our group fit the description as one of the modern sociological phenomena which joins individuals not by family, neighborhood, blood or history but by current needs or interests. In a world of increasing anonymity and mobility, it was natural that networks would proliferate as evidence of the irrepressible human need of and desire for community. Even computers and the electronic media were on the ready to connect us globally around specialized interests or viewpoints.

In our particular case, it was psychology and philosophy that unified us. History was irrelevant. In our realm only the now existed. The past was a restrictive interpretation and the future but an anxiety-ridden projection. All life was seen to be personally designed and created by each individual, moment by moment. Personal responsibility was assumed for all actions, moods, thoughts and feelings. All economic, environmental and physical conditions were accepted as chosen. Blame was eschewed. Victimhood was the most dreaded and disavowed status. In fact, victimization of any person was denied and a sometimes perversely positive interpretation was placed on all events, personal and political.

The underlying thought was that in some perhaps concealed or unknown way, the hapless players had chosen their plight which, therefore, served some ultimately good purpose. The mind was bending to believe that there were those who needed to learn about famine or lethal viruses or war or birth defects, rape, murder or death by starvation.

The daily substance of our personal lives was derided as merely our story and, yet, it became the constant subject matter of our gatherings. Obsessions with overeating, losing weight, quitting

---

[14] Marilyn Ferguson, *Aquarian Conspiracy, Personal and Social Transformation in the 1980's.* Boston: Houghton Mifflin Company, 1980.

smoking, searching for lovers and future spouses, seeking fulfilling professions, escaping a haunting sense of loneliness or depression – these were the never ending themes of our seminars and courses. Yet, these modern malaises were deemed to be erroneous and irrelevant explorations. We needed to seek after the higher calling which surely lay at the end of these fruitless quests. Each personal trial, travail or weakness we encountered had to be only a pathway to something greater than ourselves.

In the idiom of our network, we all sought enlightenment, that high form of consciousness, that connectedness with all humanity, that freedom from the petty restrictions of the ego. We viewed this state of being as an evolutionary achievement that was gained by guided introspection, group encounters and by direct involvement in humanitarian causes. We believed that our desire to achieve this exalted condition and to dedicate our lives to higher purposes set us apart from the multitudes. Many in our network zealously recruited and proselytized for one type of enlightenment course or another, seeking to achieve a kind of critical mass of similarly thinking people that, ultimately, would tilt the world toward a better destiny.

Our seminar leaders chose various causes for us to commit ourselves to as few of us had our own. Most of us had taken on the personal dedication to end hunger in the world by the year 2000, a goal instigated and recommended by one of the largest of the human potential enterprises.[15] There were, of

---

[15] The Hunger Project was dramatically launched in the 1980's to end chronic persistent hunger on the planet by the year 2000. Founders included John Denver and Werner Erhard. The program was heavily promoted within the Werner Erhard network of personal development programs. Many spin-off groups have since been launched by Hunger Project volunteers, including RESULTS, the highly effective Washington based lobbying organization begun by Sam Harris to create the political will to end hunger.

course, many individuals and established organizations pursuing the goal of a hunger-free world but, with our understanding of the true dynamics of life, we would change the paradigm. We would convert the goal of ending world hunger from a good cause to a historical inevitability.

Our thinking was simple. We believed that other well-intentioned philanthropic groups knew in their hearts that this was a lost cause and, therefore, must be taking unhealthy comfort in being attached to life's victims. We who denied the very existence of victims would transform the history and plight of mankind. After all, declaring it would make it so.

Each of us proclaimed a deeply felt desire to make a valuable contribution to other people and to the world in general whether or not we were involved in the hunger campaign. Our commitment to making a difference was not unified by a political or economic agenda. We shared no common platform of issues. What really bound us together was a personal and private quest for individual happiness. Our philanthropic activities were simply part of that pursuit.

Some observe that networks are replacing traditional organizations such as political parties or even churches for many people. Just as a church congregation can become a lynch mob when a spark ignites commonly held prejudices, networks, too, have hidden undercurrents. We who let our desire for enlightenment and contribution bring us together did not acknowledge that we were also bound by common fears, frustrations and unacknowledged needs.

On this particular evening, we were about to discover another side of ourselves and our network, the revelation of which, ultimately, ripped open our entire value system and laid waste to our relationships. We discovered that beneath the espoused goals and values we felt made us so different, more powerful forces bound us to the larger unconscious community, the very group we were trying to convert.

Abundance – The Promised Loot

If enlightenment was our salvation, abundance was our state of grace. It was an outward sign of an inner triumph. Abundance could reveal itself as a wealth of love in one's life from family and friends or in good health or fame and recognition. The surest sign, however, was financial success.

Poverty, or scarcity as it was called, was an indisputable indicator of unconsciousness, the absence of enlightenment. Abundance and scarcity were actually viewed as states of being rather than tangible conditions of life. Theoretically, a person besieged with debt and having no employment or any immediate means to create an income could enjoy a state of abundance. Conversely, an individual with a six-figure income, a home in Palm Beach, a Porsche in the driveway and substantial savings could suffer the torments of scarcity. It required an act of faith to live in abundance.

Abundance, we believed, did not necessarily require financial success. However, there was an implicit promise that the very act of faith would eventually lead to the real thing. In other words, just thinking abundance and prosperity would somehow, someday, produce a big bank account. The inevitable arrival of wealth became the abiding and unifying belief. At the foundation of this belief was the fact that each of us had, upon the release of fear and anxiety, at least once in our lives achieved success against great odds. These types of experiences were frequently recounted to bolster our faith in a destiny of wealth.

The promise that a positive mental attitude is a sure road to financial success was accompanied by an unstated but widely accepted negative corollary that those who have not achieved financial abundance live in the state of mental scarcity. Their financial difficulties are, if not the punishment for this negative and self-limiting thinking, at least, its manifestation.

Since abundance was thought to be available to all those of faith, we, the true believers, fell prey to the conviction that of all the people on earth, we were especially entitled to prosperity and abundance in our lives. The brutal reality, however, was that like nearly everyone we knew, seekers or non-seekers of enlightenment, we swam in a sea of scarcity.

Credit card payments depleted our incomes. Car payments ended only when our vehicles began falling apart. Day care expenses oppressed the many single mothers among us. Our condos were now devalued but taxes and maintenance fees were increasing yearly. Our jobs were insecure. No corporation was considered a safe haven. IBM, AT&T and Kodak were all laying off employees. Many of us who owned and managed small businesses lived through never ending cycles of near abundance only to be wiped out by unexpected downturns or cash flow crises. Some who were in professions of law, medicine or dentistry saw that overhead, insurance premiums, personnel problems and increasing competition would steal the security and independence they dreamed of. Those in secure jobs such as teaching or nursing felt grossly underpaid. Some of us, now in our 30's and even 40's, were, embarrassingly, still relying on stipends or emergency aid from our parents. The good life portrayed so vividly by Donald Trump, TV commercials, department stores and even our own seminar leaders, seemed so near and yet so very far away. The dollar was getting weaker. We were getting older.

The anxieties and pressures of these financial struggles were made all the worse by the fact that we could no longer blame or attach the cause to anyone or anything outside ourselves. We had declared ourselves ultimately and solely responsible. We were as we said "cause in the matter." We could not lament a soft real estate market, fat cats in Washington or deadbeat ex-husbands. Nor could we hope for a lucky break, a winning lotto ticket or some other turn of fate. Such dreams were only the flip side of blame, both being escapes from personal responsibility.

While taking responsibility is not blame and should have no positive or negative connotations, our Protestant, Catholic and Jewish upbringings unconsciously filtered in. The result was the merging of our New Age teachings into the hallmark of our more traditional religious backgrounds otherwise known as guilt.[16] Many of us who had been taught to feel guilty for making money now felt guilty for not making enough.

If abundance was our entitlement, was the real reason that we were not experiencing and enjoying prosperity the fact that, deep down, we had somehow chosen scarcity over plenty? Next came the thought – so, WHY do we not feel worthy, goddamit? Abundance is our right! The Universe prescribes it. We must be unconsciously resisting it. Our teachers not only urge and guide us toward it but they seem to be personally awash in money from our tuitions to their abundance courses. Would not abundance lift from our shoulders this ceaseless financial pressure that robs us of life's pleasures? Would we not more easily attain enlightenment if we were not so distracted by these bills, payments and economic uncertainties?

Unwavering faith in the creed of abundance was held by very few. Like devotees of religious groups from time immemorial, the rest of us longed to see a miracle with our own eyes. We held that abundance was our destiny and, God knows, we needed it. But, in order to maintain the faith that would keep the abundance flowing, we needed a little sign. Our souls were stained with scarcity and our lives laden with liabilities, yet we were ready for the rapture, a

---

[16] In a Johnny Carson comedy sketch, Jewish comedian David Steinberg once spoke about his mixed marriage with a Roman Catholic. "It's working pretty well," he said. "She's teaching me about shame and I am training her in guilt."

deliverance. We just needed that little portent. On this evening in February, there was talk that the sign had been given. The time for abundance to enter our lives was at hand. It only remained for us to step forward and receive it.

A Moment of Truth on the Way to Fraud and Delusion

Without a name tag[17] and despite the fact that he was unknown to most of us, we recognized that the man standing authoritatively on the stairway was one of our own — a seeker of enlightenment, committed to a better world, a colleague, a friend. After all, in our world, personal data such as occupation, age, nationality or marital status was irrelevant to defining our identities. We knew that identity was only a function of the ego which was something we were all trying to transcend.

If personal transformation could at any moment wipe out the past while recreating and redesigning one's life, weren't credentials and personal familiarity rendered meaningless pieces of information? The only pertinent moment in time, we reasoned, was in the now and the only relevant fact was that our speaker was part of our network and that he clearly spoke our language.[18]

---

[17] Part of weekend transformational programs involves the experience of having extraordinarily intimate, encounters with other seminar participants who are known only through the names tags they wear. Despite the intensity of these episodes, this intimacy generally evaporates when the course ends and the name tags come off.

[18] Transformational courses such as est (now called The Forum) or Life Spring focus attention on the present, emphasizing personal power which allows for the reinventing of one's life irrespective of culture, heredity and personal history. In a world characterized by political impotence, economic insecurity, random crime and personal alienation, the rediscovery of personal power can have an electrifying impact. In the political climate of the 1990s, this view of personal

continued on next page

He said he was a messenger, not the source. "The source resides in the benevolent Universe which takes care of all of us," he explained. "Abundance," he continued, "is our birthright but we have been resisting it." And, how well we knew it! He brought news of a system, a kind of game that could change all that. "Isn't all of life a game?" we thought. Besides, this game was founded upon infinity.

"Time as we know it," he explained, "is an illusion, a limitation which humans created and placed upon themselves. Within enlightenment there is no time. Within infinity there are no struggles, there is no competition. In reality there is plenty for us all and life is a continuous circle," he reminded us. "The game, sometimes called the Prosperity Seminar or the Infinity Game, brings abundance and prosperity to all its players. It is self-generating, an endless cycle in which participants receive and share life's bounty."

·Now we began to sigh. An end to struggle was in sight. There was no need to work as we had known it. We need only share and receive. It's available to everyone. All that is required is that we choose to participate. Wasn't this what we had all be waiting and working for? Did this not conform with our vision of how life should be? Was this not the Aquarian Age when all such phenomena would materialize? Had we not been preparing ourselves for this exact moment? Look around. The right people were gathered here to be the first to receive this secret from a loving Universe.

The messenger warned us that we would initially experience some resistance to the Infinity Game. After all, a lifetime of unworthiness is not so easily released. "But, keep in mind," he implored us, "the rewards are very, very real."

---

accountability is gaining prominence over what is now called the politics of victimization.

"How real?" we wanted to know. He announced that he himself had already received over $20,000 in less than a month. A stunned silence fell over our gathering. It took a moment for the possibility of receiving a sum of $20,000 in just one month to sink in. We saw credit card debts erased at once, cars paid for, debts to friends and family satisfied and our pride reinstated. That trip to Europe that had begun to seem unlikely would now be an absolute certainty. No more renting! We could make a down payment on a home. Our breathing became deep but rapid. A nervous energy filled our meridians. Our very chakras were pulsating. But, could this really be?

He asked those in the room who had already received gifts from the Infinity Game to stand up and testify. Several familiar faces came into view, all glowing with prosperity and smiling lovingly upon us. Each such person reported excitedly that he or she had received more than $10,000 in the last several weeks. They said it was wonderful and they wanted all of us to share in this miracle. The untroubled composure, the sublime relaxation that we all imagined would come from receiving abundance radiated from these witnesses. The credibility of our messenger, accepted without question from the beginning, now took on godlike proportions.

A stirring was felt as emotion undulated through our group. Those in the back pressed forward to hear the details more clearly. Some on the floor rearranged themselves as if preparing to rise. Eyes were wide and dilated, mouths were fixed with determination. All at once, we seemed to have acknowledged the fact that the future, which in our teens and 20's had seemed measureless, now seemed more ominous. After all, most of us had lived long enough to realize that, despite all our efforts at change and improvement, diets had failed. Rather than improve, sex and relationships seemed to have gotten more complicated. New partners or spouses had begun to, uncannily, resemble past or abandoned ones.

Despite our meditations and studies, anxious identities stared back at us from our mirrors every morning. We came on fewer and fewer answers and felt less and less enthusiasm for finding answers. We realized, in those moments, how much we despised our futile, plodding, ever-striving lifestyles, how desperately we wanted to be set free. Clearly, we had always suspected that money was our deliverance. So it was that we were ready to leave behind the pitiful lives that had trapped us within illusory walls and blinded us to the opportunities and possibilities that lay just beyond the pale of our limited vision.

YES. We were ready for deliverance. Prosperity would give us the relief we were seeking. The Infinity Game was the very answer to our prayers.

The Night – and Might – of Enrollment

To bring abundance to ourselves and, eventually, all people, the Infinity Game relied on an endless chain of enrollments and re-enrollments. This approach to achieving the evolutionary perfection of mankind was quite familiar to many in our network. We viewed ourselves as a human vanguard for enlightenment. Our mission, literally, was the salvation of the planet even as the earth faced ecological disaster or nuclear holocaust. Few of us, however, were actually environmental or peace activists. Rather, as Aquarian conspirators, we strove for a metaphysical transformation of humanity. This, we theorized, could be achieved by continuously enlisting people into our various programs, thus, enfolding them into our belief systems.

Our newfound view of life was gaining momentum in all corners of the globe. Nearly a quarter of a million people had completed the est training in America alone and it was now being delivered in Europe and Asia. Shirley MacLaine's books were being made into movies. President and Mrs. Reagan were consulting the stars. Bernie Siegel's books, placing metaphysical powers at the source of recuperation from cancer, were bestsellers. "We must have known each other in a past life" was becoming a casually accepted explanation for those moments of déja vu. Astrology, reincarnation, natural medicine, metaphysical science and transformational therapies were sweeping America and we were their standard bearers. We knew that when a critical mass was reached, we would change the course of history. This was our destiny.

At this time, the most focused proselytizers of New Age thinking were represented by various transformational personal development courses such as est, Insight and Life Spring. These were the Jesuits and the born-agains of the New Age. As a result of our involvement in any number of these human potential courses, many of us had become highly skilled in the use of enrollment techniques following the notion that enlightenment comes only through sharing and participation. That being the case, most of us had, at least once, succeeded in enrolling a friend or family member in one of our transformation programs. We witnessed, first-hand, the remarkable positive changes in their lives all of which were then attributable to our enrollment efforts.

Our enrollment zeal, however, was often compromised by a discomforting but undeniable undercurrent. Most of us had found that, shortly after taking our courses, the extraordinary breakthroughs in awareness and the energizing new perspectives that we gained seemed to rapidly dissipate. We also began to notice that these troubling letdowns could be somewhat lessened or even delayed by our efforts to enroll others in these very same programs. Somehow, by enthusiastically recalling and discussing some of our wondrous experiences, the life-changing phenomenon was relived and the euphoria extended.[19]

Those of us who had dropped out of transformational programs and self-development courses for extended periods of time usually experienced a period of depression which brought about a sense of emptiness and a return to hated personal habits of overeating, overworking or staring

---

[19] A common and unifying experience of many in the New Age community is the euphoric sense of freedom and joy that results from a transformational or human potential program. More than a million people in the U.S. have now participated in such courses, experiencing graduation nights filled with ecstasy and celebration and the commonly resultant desire to love and embrace one's fellowmen now seen as simply trapped within the same bonds that had previously held one's self.

dumbly at the television. However, by re-enrolling in such programs, we were able to regain our sense of purpose and fight off our negative proclivities.

Enrollment events were regularly sponsored by many human potential programs. Those of us who attended these high energy rallies were led in hand-clapping, laughing sessions which focused on people testifying to the benefits they had gained from the courses. In our reborn excitement, we engaged invited guests in conversations, urging them to sign up for seminars and workshops. We asked the well-taught, penetrating questions that were designed to lead the guests to see how such programs would benefit their lives, most particularly, when vulnerable and unsatisfying areas of life were exposed.

Few of us realized it at the time, but this approach is one of the most powerful of all direct sales closing techniques and the ability to successfully use it accounts for the arrogant swagger of many a salesman. Once armed with the knowledge of a prospect's admitted needs or desires, the salesman has only through power of persuasion to link his product to the fulfillment of those expressed needs.[20]

After these experiences, enrollment as the basis of the Infinity Game seemed natural, acceptable and achievable. To make things even easier to explain and more fun, posited the messenger, the enrollment process of the Game used a little analogy that was based on the airline industry. Hence, the Infinity Game became more popularly known as the Airplane Game.

Here's how it went. We were asked to imagine a planeload of people consisting of eight passengers,

---

[20] In encyclopedia sales, the salesperson is trained to elicit the parents' hopes and dreams for their children's futures. Once acknowledged, the reference books are shown as the key to the fulfillment of those hopes. The interpretation is that failure to buy the books means that the parents are uncaring or, even worse, obstructing or damaging the children's future well-being.

four crew members, two co-pilots and, at the top, the pilot. One would become a player in the Airplane Game by gifting the pilot $1,500 to gain a seat on the plane. When the eight seats had been filled by passengers each having given the pilot $1,500, the pilot left the game or "piloted out."

When the pilot did so, the airplane split into two with the previous two co-pilots now advancing to pilot status. In accordance with this split, the previous four crew members now also split and advanced to co-pilot status on the two new planes. The previous eight passengers were divided into two crews of four, each with the assignment to enroll eight new passengers in order to continue the Game. With each enrollment of sixteen new people into the Game, this same split would occur. And, so it went.

Now that the Game was understood, it was also clear that the sensible thing to do seemed to be to repeatedly pilot-out and re-enter as a passenger on another plane. As this type of self-styled frequent flyer, one had the opportunity to receive unlimited returns on an initial $1,500 investment simply by continuing to re-enter. This was the way in which the messenger had received his $20,000 and the witnesses their $10,000 all in less than a month. This was the key to their exultation and accompanying radiant states of abundance.

It was all about getting people to join the Game so we could spread the prosperity, one person at a time. We got it. In fact, due to prior training, we had already accepted enrollment as a way of life. We knew that without continuous enrollment, without the constant selling of our so-called transformational experiences, our personal lives somehow lost luster leaving room for mischief and malignancy to insidiously re-appear.

Enrollment was simply a method of sharing life's greatest secrets. Why, humanity could actually be said to be dependent upon it in light of the life-giving benefits we had witnessed among those who had participated in programs as a result of our sign-up efforts. It was no surprise, then, that we came to believe that we had yet another secret, perhaps the most potent of all. As we now understood it, enrollment led to not only enlightenment and happiness but to great financial abundance. We had always known that abundance was our destiny, therefore, it was perfectly understandable to us that the Universe would design a means by which to spread our beneficent message and allow us to make lots of money at the same time. Clearly, enrollment was fused to abundance.

Following the presentation by the messenger and an explanation of the Game's metaphysical principles, the outpouring of participation from those in attendance was explosive. Existing pilots were identified and they quickly broke off into small gatherings to organize enrollments and systems of support. Within fifteen minutes, some of us had advanced to crew level. Those who were too incredulous or short of funds were, eventually, enrolled by supporters who double- or triple-teamed them, overcoming objections with compassionate advice.

A new party line was instantly established through direct and probing questions. Are you afraid of prosperity? Do you want to suffer the rest of your life? Can you not accept that the Universe loves you? Are you holding onto scarcity so you don't have to deal with your real goals? Don't be afraid. Prosperity will help you attain them. Then came the coup de grâce. Surely there is someone you can borrow the money from, someone who wants to see you have it all!

A mesmerizing and compelling force enveloped our gathering. Not one person challenged the messenger or even asked a pointed question about the Game. Obviously, we had been well-prepared for this electrifying moment. Neither doubt nor objection entered our minds.

Instead, now committed to the Game, we thrust ourselves forward into a torrent of evangelical action. Embracing every new instruction as if each would lead to the unfolding of a perfect universal order, we accepted the edict that all transactions in the Airplane Game were to be made in cash, preferably in $100 bills. We raptly listened to the messenger depict, in thrilling detail, the healthful benefits and resultant fun of receiving all those C-notes. "Hold and caress those bills," he advised as excellent therapy for releasing any negative energy or thoughts of scarcity.

No money was allowed to be transacted at the meeting itself, only afterwards as a private affair between new passengers and their,pilots. After all, the money was a gift and should be treated as such. We were advised that it might just add to our own future prosperity if we enclosed the money in an envelope with a card bearing a heartfelt personal message of love and support. Thus it was that seeming tongues of fire descended upon our group that evening in February inspiring us with the miraculous message of the Airplane Game.

Next, we discovered that an alias would abet the cause. Yes, in keeping with the metaphysical nature of this process, the messenger offered another rule of the Game – that we refrain from using our given names. Rather, we were urged to adopt an enlightened title, something that reflected our highest values and our deepest longings. We were told to take on a name that reflected our very souls. Thus it was that Truth & Joy embraced Heavenly Pursuit and Heightened Endeavor pledged support and loyalty to Serenity.

The Airplane Game

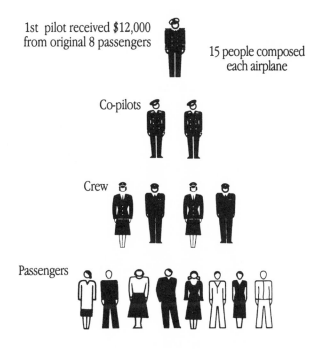

1st pilot received $12,000
from original 8 passengers

15 people composed
each airplane

Co-pilots

Crew

Passengers

These first passengers each paid $1,500 to the Pilot and
the first split occurred.

Then a series of further splits occurred that divided the planes into
halves and each half recruited eight people in order to divide again.
Three splits were needed for each level of passengers to reach the
pilot level

The Days After the Night Before

In the days and evenings following that transformational first meeting, visits were made to banks and credit unions for withdrawals of crisp, new $100 bills. In parking lots, at restaurants and bars or in the privacy of living rooms, Honesty slipped Integrity a plain white envelope. Loyalty held a rendezvous with Love & Happiness. Commitment hugged Excellence then lovingly placed a package in her pocket. Velocity gifted Courage with what looked like a thick greeting card. Then, out we went to enjoin family and friends to take seats as passengers on various planes.

It seemed that the dreary days of struggle brought on by scarcity thinking and unfounded hope had ended. The much-awaited transformation had occurred. After years of oversleeping and awakening in groggy stupors, many of us upon enrolling in the Game began arising at 6 a.m. feeling alert and expectant. The dulling habits of Happy Hour drinking, eating evening snacks and sweets were put aside. Diets were unnecessary, alcohol or drugs unwanted distractions. Infused with a new joy of life, we had no need for such indulgences. Adrenaline was now our fix.

Old fears of calling people or reluctance to approach friends with new ideas or invitations vanished. We spontaneously contacted fellow players throughout the day with encouragement and reports of successful enrollments. We phoned relatives, old lovers, ex-wives and friends whom we had not seen or spoken with in years. Suddenly, they were remembered as obvious new beneficiaries of the bounty that was flowing.

Naturally, our first contacts were directed at fellow seekers of enlightenment, those graduates and perennial seminar enlistees of all those human potential and New Age courses. Meetings for groups of three to five planes were held three nights a week in the homes of pilots. Potential passengers were brought to hear the word and experience the

Aquarian energy. Many of us whose days and nights had seemed so perpetually crowded, stretched and incomplete, now, amazingly, found our evenings available for these inspiring and euphoric gatherings. Illusion though it was, time had miraculously expanded.

Many of us went from passenger to crew to co-pilot in just two weeks, just as promised. Pilot status and that gift of $10,500 profit lay just ahead. A delicious giddiness possessed us affecting all areas of our lives. It was a little like being in love. Sex was thrilling. Food was ambrosial. Florida's winter skies were ever more cobalt, the white billowy clouds taking on mythical shapes that seemed to outline our dreams and goals. Life, once so predictable and laborious, was now magically infused with wonder.

Our enrollment meetings were boisterous and ebullient. We just knew that coveted pilot status, like enlightenment itself, might be only one meeting away. Each new enrollment moved us closer to that ultimate goal. Even better was the knowledge that once pilot status was achieved and the gift received, the process could begin again. If $10,000 could eliminate debt from our lives, surely $20,000 would ensure our cherished goals. The lifestyles of some of the recycled pilots became models to emulate. Several arrived at meetings in new BMWs which they announced had been made possible by the Game. "Everyone on earth should own a BMW," they would joke. "The Universe wants it that way!" New homes were being purchased. Diamonds were displayed on the fingers of once doubtful but now triumphant wives and girlfriends. Extravagant vacations were being planned. But, while the momentum was growing, no one was going anywhere. Someday there would be time for holidays but, for now, life was too thrilling and fully-satisfying to even indulge in dream trips.

Doubts, accusations or warnings were issued by family or friends who saw our lives becoming possessed by the Game. They were simply brushed aside as having been delivered by the unenlightened.

People who refused to play were branded scarcity thinkers, afraid of life itself or just not smart enough to understand what they were being offered.

Our private thoughts reflected the fact that we now believed their financial struggles or personal problems were self-induced. Certainly, becoming a part of the Airplane Game was the solution. It verified everything we had learned in all those seminars – that prosperity is the very will of the Universe and that this simple vehicle was being offered as the means towards banishing all malevolent influences from our pasts.

Those jobs and businesses once seen as stressful and time consuming miraculously expanded to allow for daily phoning to players and prospects, private support conferences and evening rallies. Sales calls were deferred, appointments put off, reports postponed, patients and clients re-scheduled. Priorities were quickly rearranged as we acknowledged that few of us could make $10,000 even in two months at our current careers. Placing our jobs on hold was economically justified. In fact, the Game was far more interesting and rejuvenating than anything our work offered anyway.

We had learned our seminar lessons well. Life was supposed to be fun! The choice, on a metaphysical level, was obvious. This was IT and nothing could distract us.

When in Doubt, Deny

From the beginning there were doubters but their questions were summarily dismissed by the devoted, their reticence dogmatically interpreted as fear. Infused with faith, we had little tolerance for non-believers. Obviously, those poor souls were just not players in life. In fact, those who could not be enrolled were viewed as handicapped, unenlightened, committed to scarcity.

On the other hand, players were seen as the chosen ones of the Universe. All that was required to obtain life's abundance was a willingness to share, risk, support and to be a little intrusive with our mission. Nonetheless, after several unforgettable weeks of zeal for enrollment and our bigoted dismissal of skeptics, the crusade seemed to have nearly exhausted the ranks of the enlightenment seekers.

As intended, the Game was now reaching out to new levels of society with its providential influence. But, the entry of a later class of passengers began to provoke some unsettling feelings among the faithful. There seemed to be a qualitative difference between the first disciples and the new enrollees.

It was not faith in abundance that had attracted these new supporters but unabashed lust at the sight of real cash, new cars and jewelry. Some of the newest passengers already wore heavy gold jewelry at their open-collared shirts. Many were older and, rather than coming from the elite professional and managerial ranks, these were, well, the types of people one might also see hanging around the race track!

Not transformationalists dedicated to redeeming mankind, they, instead, seemed to exude the faults that the initiates were trying to eliminate from the world – insatiable acquisitiveness, predatory competition, control, power. So what were they doing in this Infinity Seminar? And, what, asked the enlightened with greater alarm, were they doing with them?

For the first time, an ugly word began to be heard around the Game. Greed. Curiously, this word was still not applied to the charter members but was only brought to mind by the language, posture and appearance of the newest passengers who were not naming themselves Harmony, Health or Hugs but, rather, Stingray, Top Gun and Goldfinger.

Clearly a qualitative shift had occurred and the beatific attitudes so prevalent in those early evening gatherings had now been replaced by get-down-to-business glares and salacious smiles. Gone was the innocent giddiness, the warm and loving camaraderie. Instead, people now huddled together, conspiratorially plotting stealthy strategies to compound earnings.

A new strategy emerged as people began sponsoring passengers who came with no money to invest. When these not-at-risk players piloted out, they would give back to the sponsor the initial stake of $1,500 plus half the abundance they had received in gifts. Some ambitious pilots, after receiving their eight gifts of $1,500 each, re-invested portions of their returns to acquire subsidiaries, then took seats on their very own planes. With such continued momentum, an enterprising pilot could within weeks receive as much as $25,000 rather than the measly $10,500 he would have obtained by simply re-enrolling.

As this sponsorship strategy created a new class of player, the relationships among participants changed drastically. New passengers making $1,500 payments to sponsoring pilots were, in fact, giving half of these gifts to unnamed financial backers which seriously distorted the intended sentiment. After all, how would one send a loving card to a silent investor? It was a gesture as hollow as sending a greeting card to one's bank.

Although bearing similarities to a franchise, this sponsorship arrangement was, in actuality, more like indentured servitude. The sponsored person might turn out to be a poor supporter on his plane, enrolling no one and offering nothing by way of encouragement to other players. He might just go along for the ride and collect his $5,250 at the end. Players might now demand that the sponsor require more participation from those that he sponsored. In the worst case, a sponsor could summarily dismiss his or her stand-ins and replace them with others who were more cooperative.

Certain sponsors were beginning to look like loan sharks, wheeling and dealing in human cargo on the planes. They no longer joined arm-in-arm with fellow passengers, crew and co-pilots to find abundance through enrollment. Instead, they dropped in at evening meetings to check on the status of their investments and monitored subsidized passengers with daily calls from their newly purchased car phones.

You Can Run But You Can't Hide

While the Game was sometimes called the Infinity Game, the Prosperity Seminar, or, more commonly, the Airplane Game, one particular word had been assiduously avoided in its description. That word was pyramid as in pyramid scheme. In truth, most players knew that pyramid schemes were fraudulent and illegal. But the concept lived in a fuzzy realm far removed from their daily lives. As a fraudulent and illegal activity, the pyramid scheme was associated with crooks and liars, people without integrity. As it was understood, a pyramid was instigated and manipulated by one person who profited enormously at the pitiable expense of a multitude of victims.

Bathing in abundance, surrounded by well-meaning and highly-evolved friends and colleagues, this term had no reference to the charter members of the Game. Clearly, there were no victims in this Game. In fact, we all knew there were no victims in life, period. The community of newly-prosperous pilots was growing. There was no one person scamming the rest. If the messenger had received generously, well, so had many others.

Now, however, some of the most recent entrants to the Game were casually saying that they knew it was a pyramid. But, it didn't matter as long as one got in early enough. Their only worry was that the Game would end before they reached pilot level.

End? What did they mean, end? None of the earliest players had even considered that the Airplane Game would end. Didn't they get it? Infinity doesn't end. This was about continuous re-enrollments. And, even if there were a finite level of enrollment due to the intransigence of the unenlightened, the surface of South Florida had barely been scratched.

Yes, rumors had begun to circulate that the Game was technically illegal due to some obscure state laws written by legislators who could not possibly understand what they were outlawing. Anyway, the Game's legality had not been challenged. And, it was ridiculous to think that something so good could possibly be banned.

The mercenary attitude of the newest passengers was quite disturbing. Association with them along with a rising awareness of crass commercialism among some of the enlightened suggested further troubling aspects for many of the participants. Here then were uncomfortable reminders of another known metaphysical law which was a fundamental precept of all those seminars: The world always mirrors our inner selves. Therefore, what is conspicuous in others is actually a reflection of what lies within us.

The enlightened individual took due notice of this phenomenon at all times and used it as a monitor of his inner being. The question, then, had to be why were the loving, sharing, enlightened members of the Airplane Game seeing greed, selfishness, scheming and ignorance all around them? If the law was, indeed, immutable, the answer was becoming more painfully clear.

Threatened with doubts and questions about pyramids, rapacious and exploitative behavior, illegalities and outright fraud, the surprising response was to numb the mind of worries and engage in further flurries of enrollment all the while enjoying the delicious anticipation of abundance.

The Ignorant, the Accused and the Arrested

It was six weeks into the Game when the insinuated, rumored and avoided became real. Placed deep within the local section, one of South Florida's largest daily papers ran a small article in which a sheriff's office asserted that the Airplane Game was an illegal pyramid scheme. It warned that investors were guilty of misdemeanor and subject to fine and imprisonment. The spokesman said the sheriff's office had received numerous complaints from people who claimed to have been solicited to participate. The article was received with stunned amazement and embarrassment by zealous players.

The common thought was that this had to be some monstrous mistake or some equally hideous display of gross ignorance. Coming from faceless authorities as a direct accusation and backed with the naked threat of imprisonment, it felt like persecution of the just by paranoid or malevolent powers. After all, authorities have a history of attacking bold new thinking. New forms of art and literature have historically suffered the suppression of established powers when first introduced.

Then a follow-up article of about the same size carried a statement from the State Attorney General's office that the Airplane Game violated the state lottery law. Players were threatened with jail. But the State of Florida itself ran a lottery! The hypocrisy was truly amazing.

Some radical players speculated that the very structure of government was threatened by the potential of the Airplane Game. Think about it. If abundance was available to all, much of government bureaucracy would become even more unnecessary. Welfare would disappear. Social Security would be pointless. And, so the argument went.

The fact that a state which ran and promoted a public lottery could be accusing honest citizens of running an illegal one was sufficient to discredit the published articles along with the quoted officials. The Florida Lottery posted odds of 14 million-to-one for winning. Yet, television stations, government officials and the major newspapers promoted the State Lottery as if winning was as likely as getting an unexpected phone call from an old friend.

Further, a large constituency of Florida's Lottery was made up of the poor and the disenfranchised. So great was the seduction of the Lottery for this group that some small churches in poor communities complained that since the Lottery's inception their own revenues had suffered markedly.

It was the beneficiaries of this regressive, deceitful program who now pointed an accusatory finger at the Game's benevolent system. Their use of inappropriate terms like investors and solicitations and their comparisons of the Infinity Seminar to games of chance proved it. So, with truth on our side, we defiantly though nervously marched forward with scheduled meetings, renewed enrollments and even greater dedication.

A week after the repudiated charges of illegality had been printed, we awoke to find our Game again reported in the newspaper. However, this time the article was not insignificant or buried near the obituaries. It was no longer a warning of technical illegality. This time, there was a long and prominent account of the police entering private homes, demanding identification from players and arresting pilots.

"PYRAMID SUSPECTS ARRESTED!" the headline screamed. The names of those arrested were listed as if they were common bank robbers. According to the article, they were "leaders of the scheme and were charged with conducting an illegal lottery." It stated that the police had received numerous complaints from people "bilked in the scheme" and the object of the Game was referred to as "get rich quick." It called those exhilarating and boisterous enrollment gatherings "secret meetings." An undercover deputy who had been posted near one of the meetings for surveillance described the arrival of our enlightened players as "quail coming home to roost." The story told how use of the mail was deliberately avoided and that participants used aliases. These tactics, the article implied, were designed solely to evade the law.

Players were called promoters and described as traveling from county to county seeking innocent recruits. The Game or close variations of it had swept through the universities of Florida and South Florida, the article explained. Gainesville police said as many as 1,000 University of Florida students had taken part.

In the following days, several more articles appeared, each reporting new arrests and describing the Infinity Seminar in the terminology of criminal fraud. Enrollees were identified as victims. Pilots were called ringleaders. The promise of receiving $12,000 for a $1,500 initial investment was presented as a preposterous come-on, an insidious trap. The investigators and arresting officers were from the Organized Crime Unit of a city police department and from the State Attorney's office. This was a crackdown!

Spokesmen for the police said they were making the arrests to warn investors away from the Game and to make it clear that it was strictly illegal. Those arrested were charged with first degree misdemeanor. They were taken away from the meetings to police stations, finger-printed, charged then released to appear before a judge at a scheduled hearing.

Paranoia and fear now seized many who had finally attained pilot status a goal that had been so pleasurably anticipated and, until this day, joyously celebrated. A creeping sense of guilt sucked out our enthusiasm. The meetings we had so enjoyed now appeared treacherous. The thoughts of police stealthily lying in wait, of being placed under surveillance or of being entrapped by undercover agents converted the entire Game into a web of intrigue, starkly in contrast to the sunny optimism and mutual support that had previously characterized our involvement. The Game which we had viewed as an avant-garde movement for prosperity and freedom now loomed as a dangerous enterprise threatening imprisonment and humiliation. A sickening anxiety took possession of our spirits. The question was how could this have happened? And, how in the world could true seekers of spirituality have created this?

The camaraderie, the late night phone calls of encouragement, the support system which had led to a wonderful sense of belonging to a good cause were all being replaced by a sense of panic and a desire to go into hiding. Pride was being displaced by even more intense feelings of guilt and shame.

Several pilots held re-grouping sessions so that players could express their feelings and begin to cope with recent events. The evasive tactics that Game players had been accused of using – changing meeting times and locations at the last minute, avoiding use of the mail and real names and other tools of the real criminal underground – were now being deliberately employed. Participants were interviewed at the door for credentials and references. The connectedness, that source of group strength and effectiveness, now seemed a dangerous liability.

At one meeting, participants were advised to envision themselves naked, bathing in dollar bills, to imagine having all the money they needed, to picture having the car or boat or clothes they wanted. These images, they were told, should now be conjured up in order to counteract the negativity that had been manifested. The meeting leaders confirmed that it was, indeed, the players themselves who had created the police. Then, without missing a beat, they said that the only thing that could really threaten the Game was an interruption of enrollments. Attendees at the meeting confessed a gut-wrenching fear, a dizzying confusion.

Why, then, was the Game being called a fraud? Why were people being persecuted? And, was the Game really worth risking incarceration and a ruined reputation?

Yes, they answered. Yet, as the shaken members left, hurrying to their cars while looking furtively left and right, they knew it wasn't. In fact, it was over and the truth was that these players never wanted to see or hear from each other again even as they smiled like insurance salesmen, hugged at the door and quickly departed.

Descent Into Awareness

After going back to work, skipping the first scheduled enrollment meeting or quietly sitting at home without phone interruptions from supporters, those despicable words began running through our minds. "Fraud, scheme, pyramid, get-rich-quick, bilked, victims, lottery." The images of pilots being led away in shame and confusion were vivid and frightening.

One critical question, however, remained unanswered. It concerned this pyramid structure and the matter of its being able to be mathematically sustained. Strangely, the news articles did not directly address this issue. Was it to avoid comparison to the State Lottery's own arithmetical deception? Whatever the odds were of becoming a pilot, they were surely better than 14 million-to-one!

In fact, anyone who had attended an enrollment meeting knew or had met numerous people who had reached pilot status and had actually received hard, cold cash. If people were, in fact, deriving the promised rewards, why would the police barge in and attack the Game telling people they would lose their money?

From Palm Beach to Miami in the days following these arrests, a few finally took up pencil and paper and began honestly plotting the numbers that would have been required for the Game to continue, assuming its protection from the law.

To this point unshaken by the gross avarice of later enrollees and unfazed by the ridicule or reticence of non-players throughout the weeks of participation, it was only in these private, awful moments that our faith was finally shattered. For in the pure and logical clarity which only mathematics can provide, the perverse numerical symmetry of a pyramid sales organization was finally exposed. The Game was, indeed, up.

Revelation began with a look at the pyramid calculations starting with the first pilot who needed just eight passengers in order to gain his abundance. Those first eight needed just 64 new enrollments in order to achieve their prosperity. When those 64 became pilots, they had to find 512 (64 x 8) new passengers who, in turn, needed 4,096 (512 x 8) enrollees. Assuming, as we did, that the entire Universe was available for transformation and noting the rate at which we were enrolling new players, these numbers had not seemed daunting. In fact, an infinite future for the Game had at this point seemed entirely feasible. So far, so good.

Now the Game began proceeding through a series of splits. After joining the Game as a passenger and filling the other seven seats, pilots were exiting and planes were splitting in two, advancing passengers to crew membership on one of two new planes. Each plane which consisted of a pilot, two co-pilots and four crew members for a total of seven, now set about filling its eight vacant passenger seats. When that was achieved, the plane split again advancing crew members to co-pilot status of yet another craft. Four of the recently enrolled passengers became crew and all team members set out to enroll another eight more players. When that was achieved, co-pilots finally advanced to pilot status. After eight more passengers came aboard the new plane, the pilot received the promised money and the plane split into halves once again.

From the time one joined as a passenger, four splits were needed in order for that player to receive money then either leave the Game or rejoin another plane as a new passenger. Some planes had greater momentum and split more quickly than others. It was conceivable that a plane, due to the lack of effort of the players, might not enroll enough new passengers in which case it would crash and burn. Prior to the police crack down, there were no reports of failed planes.

Every plane in the Game had its genesis in the original plane established in South Florida. This potent and regenerative first aircraft had been created by the messenger. He had personally assembled a team of co-pilots and crew and had begun soliciting paying passengers. Split one had resulted in two new planes. Split two resulted in four and so on. Although by then some planes had advanced to further stages, on an overall basis, the Game had reached split number 10.

Even with clumsy computation, one could roughly calculate that after 10 consecutive splits originating from that first plane, there would be 1,024 planes in existence. All the planes assembled, each with a pilot, two co-pilots and four crew members, would have included a total of 7,168 participants. All of these planes were now seeking eight new players for an aggregate total of 8,192 additional participants. If they all achieved that goal, there would be at least 15,360 players in the whole Game throughout South Florida. To this point, still in the realm of the believable.

This was a very conservative estimate of total participation based on a general sense of the number of meetings we had heard about and the levels of attendance. However, the grapevine had it that there were not 1,000 individual pilots. In fact, high levels of re-entry by previous pilots along with sponsorship activity had reduced the total number of beneficiaries to, perhaps, only several hundred. At the point of split number 10, more than one thousand pilot seats existed, possibly many more.

A simple multiplication of this number by $12,000 (8 x $1,500) for each passenger seat revealed a potential gross revenue of over $12 million. So, in less than eight weeks, the Game had gained the power to generate nearly $12 million for just a few hundred people. The earliest players had been in the uniquely fortuitous position through re-entry and sponsorships to reap extraordinary returns in a very short period of time. Several of the earliest and most enterprising pilots had reportedly garnered more than $100,000 each.

Plunging into mathematical revelations like moths toward a flame, the question now was, if ten splits produced 1,024 planes, how many planes would exist when split number 20 occurred? Proceeding step-by-step on pocket calculators or on scraps of paper, the number was finally generated – 1,480,576. Doubling each time a split occurred resulted in an astronomical increase of airplanes after the first stages of growth. But, focusing on the immutable laws of metaphysics, no one had even considered the simple principles of mathematics.

In hindsight, the scam was revealed. More than 10 splits had occurred in approximately eight weeks of the Game's inception. To maintain the same momentum in just two more months, over 8 million people would have to have been enrolled in order to fill more than one million planes. If, in fact, this Herculean feat had been accomplished, there would have been a total of fifteen million players or far more people than live in the entire state of Florida, counting every nursing home resident, new born infant and illegal alien.

Not in complexity but in sheer magnitude, the computation went beyond the capacity of most small calculators – 8,053,063,608! Far more than the population of the entire earth, would have been needed to fill those planes! Infinity, indeed.

Faced with the enormity and implausibility of achieving such numbers and in the face of any previous sense of this as a reality, many of us finally saw that this was all about a pitiably brief and feeble human enterprise which was destined to fall apart under its own weight. The police did not have to break up the Airplane Game. It was already collapsing along with our futile dreams and pathetic beliefs.

By the end of the Game in 1987, the total Airplane Game constituency from the cities of Jupiter to Miami was conservatively estimated at 15,000. The Game resembled an explosive new company with sales doubling every few weeks and revenues approaching $12 million a month. With equal speed within the two weeks following news reports and actual arrests, the product was publicly discredited, the organization shattered and every participant threatened with jail.

Only a tiny fraction of the Game's players actually faced the bitter reality of the now obvious flimflam. A few placed head in hand, grasping both the tragedy and the comedy of having been lured into a classic scam by their own larceny. Many who understood this truth went through complex emotional reactions as they looked with sickened hearts at how little they had actually concerned themselves with the welfare of the family members, friends and colleagues whom they had enrolled.

Reflecting on how they had forsaken professional and family responsibilities during this frantic, greedy, dreamlike period, they looked within themselves to find the source of this strange behavior. What could have led deeply caring, sensitive and honorable people to this foolish and embarrassing position?

Ultimately, participation in the Game had compromised the very assets that the participants had claimed were non-negotiable, beyond any price – friendship, integrity, honor, family. It was as if Infinity had diabolically tested their souls and found them purchasable for $10,500.

The dishonesty of the Game was now so painfully obvious that any protestations of ignorance lacked credibility. It was preposterous to claim that it had really been about selflessly trying to spread prosperity rather than seizing it all at the expense of others.

We had been like children who gleefully choose the million dollars when asked the riddle – "Which would you rather have, a penny that doubles every day for a month or a million dollars right now?" – not realizing that the first penny would grow to over $10 million in just 30 days.

The riddle fools children not because they are unaware of mathematical principles but because they are easily distracted by the fantasy of a million dollars. That same desire to grab for the immediate reward, initially a mere $10,500, led the players of the Airplane Game to ignore not only their mathematical skills but their innermost urgings as well. The greatest irony was that it was the government, that very bastion of unenlightenment, that finally stopped the madness.

When the police broke the Game apart, ten to twenty thousand more people were on their way to losing their $1,500 investments. The police intervention reduced the number of losers but, had they not suppressed the Game, it was certainly on its way to collapse. The Game did not have to surpass the number of people on earth or even South Florida to fall apart. It just had to reach a point where getting eight passengers to fill the seats was a time consuming and difficult process, a point it had already begun to reach.

Mystical Mathematics

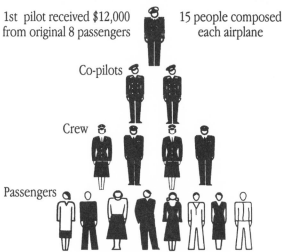

1st pilot received $12,000
from original 8 passengers

15 people composed
each airplane

Co-pilots

Crew

Passengers

These first passengers each paid $1,500 to the Pilot and
the first split occurred.

Then a series of further splits occurred that divided the planes into
halves and each half recruited eight people in order to divide again.
Three splits were needed for each level of passengers to reach the
pilot level.

		Additional people recruited	Total number of players	Total number of pilots	Total dollars involved
Split	# 2	1 6	3 1	3	$36,000
Split	# 3	3 2	6 3	7	$84,000
Split	# 4	6 4	127	1 5	$180,000
Split	# 5	128	255	3 1	$372,000
Split	# 6	256	511	6 3	$756,000
Split	# 7	512	1,023	127	$1,524,000
Split	# 8	1,024	2,047	255	$3,060,000
Split	# 9	2,048	4,095	511	$6,132,000
Split	#10	4,096	8,191	1,023	$12,276,000
Split	#11	8,092	16,383	2,047	$24,564,000
Split	#12	16,384	32,767	4,095	$49,140,000
Split	#13	32,768	65,535	8.091	$97,092,000
Split	#14	65,536	131,071	16,383	$196,596,000
Split	#15	131,072	262,143	32,767	$393,204,000
Split	#16	262,144	524,287	65,535,	$786,420,000
Split	#17	524,288	1,048,575	131,071	$1,572,852,000
Split	#18	1,048,576	2,097,151	262,143	$3,145,716,000
Split	#19	2,097,152	4,194,303	524,287	$6,291,444,000
Split	#20	4,194,304	8,388,607	1,048,575	$12,582,900,000

The Sorrowful Outcome.

It became painfully obvious that the best spiritual principles had been applied to justify and undergird a classic confidence game. Participants and observers could only wonder what all that said about such principles. Were they faulty or were there other far more powerful forces at work?

At this shattering moment, however, many of us grasped for reasons for our criminal behavior, instinctively wanting to believe that we had not gone astray at all. Like all lawbreakers, we tried to convince ourselves that we had done wrong for good reasons. We were going to be winners in life and wasn't that preferable to losing? Wasn't prosperity a goal worthy of our highest priority? The possibility, even probability, of immediate and great financial success had been regularly depicted in newspapers, magazines and television. One radio station in the area continuously played excerpts from audio tapes of success masters. This motivational station told us that success was always within our grasp. The key was in our own attitude. The need for long, plodding years of hard work was made obsolete by the recent breakthroughs in our understanding of the subconscious. We could literally attract success by training our subconscious mind with positive affirmations.

As to the victims, well, unlike in most scams where there is a perpetrator and a so-called victim, in this Game all of the participants had became perpetrators. Even those who had spent years exploring the realms of self-actualization and inner awareness were obviously acting out of clearly unexamined beliefs and feelings.

It was not surprising, then, that while a few looked directly into the ugliness of their greedy participation in the Game, many more struggled to rationalize it. In the final days, some players actually refused to desist. The fiercely aggressive ones, most of whom were near pilot status, declared that the police action was only a manifestation of the group's own fears and negativity. They said to quit would only solidify such cancerous inclinations and that the only cure was to play on, to enroll even more people.

Some went on to do so although a few admitted experiencing a sense of theft after recruiting that next player and receiving the $1,500 enrollment fee. Ironically, they attributed their sense of thievery not to the action itself or to any evaluation of their own morality but rather to having absorbed the other person's fear during the exchange.

The whole experience bears out how correctly it is said that, "Whom the gods would destroy, they first make crazy." Certainly that's what was seen in those final days of the Airplane Game where, as police stalked the meetings, many of the newly-rich pilots brazenly entered another $5,000 Super Game which promised pilots a return of $40,000. As in the lower cost game, it was the wily originators who profited enormously from this final debacle. The rest threw away their money in what almost seemed a final, ritualized indiscretion.

The Game, much like the shark who has to keep moving or drown, actually died not from suppression but from inertia as fear and greed played tug-of-war with the souls of unhappy enrollees. Some former pilots were plagued with guilt over having abandoned thousands who had lost their money. Many players agonized over phone calls from the most recently enrolled participants who begged for the return of their money or challenged them to continue the Game so they would not lose their investments.

On the other hand, there were winners who counted their blessings as they hid their abundance in safe deposit boxes out of the reach of IRS auditors. They simply took refuge in the American business maxim – if it makes money, it must be all right. In a final rationale, they asked themselves – was this really so different than getting out of the stock market just before a crash?

As for those thousands who lost their $1,500 after being told that the Game was an infinite system of sharing, well, they were now on their own and needed to take full responsibly for their own situations. The topnote of this arrogant and sorrowful aftermath was captured in the attitude of players who looked at those arrested and other losers as having created their own demises in order to have the opportunity to correct subtle malefactions in their own characters. One former pilot who was arrested in Florida offered this overview of his experience.

"Looking back, I view the whole experience as a personal development tool, an intense microcosm of my whole life. I piloted out the first time in one week and then just kept playing and piloting out several more times. It was an experience in which, for the first time in my life, I felt included in something larger than me. I didn't have to push this Game. It was sucking me in. The energy of the people, the meetings, the conversations, it all felt positive, life supporting. It was wonderful.

"Then the energy changed from joy to fear and greed. It got ugly. It was a challenge for us all to hold on to the highest thought. Many of us did not. It was our change of heart that brought in the media attention and then the police. The media involvement was a challenge to us all to face down our own demons.

"After the articles appeared in the paper calling the Game an illegal fraud, we began to take on the fear of those who read the articles. We began to process their fear, to feel what they were feeling. Getting the $1,500 gifts began to feel like stealing. For myself, I know that I attracted the police to me from my own fear. I brought them to me.

"My phone was ringing off the hook before I got arrested with people trying to get their money back. As soon as my name appeared in the paper, they quit calling me. Maybe they were afraid my phone was bugged. In any event, they left me alone and that was a relief.

"All in all, it was worth the experience. I did make quite a lot of money. I was one of those out of the thousands who played who got arrested. So I paid my dues. I don't owe anybody anything. I know it's called a fraud but everything is a fraud. Banks are frauds. The stock market is a fraud. The Game is illegal because the government doesn't get any of the money, that's all. I never coerced anyone to play. If they lost their money, it's not my responsibility. There were no victims in the Airplane Game. It was four years ago, I really don't think about it much any more."

His last comment may have been the most interesting. "No, I won't get near multi-level marketing. I don't like the smell."

Regarding those who were arrested, they, too, were just acting out their own karmas and could now have the benefit of a rare and insightful experience if they simply had the courage to look at it that way. The ordeal of having their names in the paper as ringleaders of a fraud, of being forcibly taken to a police station and finger-printed, of being marched in front of a judge who publicly chastised them and sentenced them to community service work – all of this must have manifested to show them certain negative and self-destructive thoughts that they had been harboring.

With such maneuverings of logic and philosophic thought, those who were not arrested exonerated themselves then righteously, if not compassionately, dismissed the plight of their disgraced cohorts. Some who were arrested after having acquired tens of thousands of dollars in the Game viewed the arrest as a clearing away of any personal culpability.

False Profits

The Case For Responsibility

The Airplane Game pyramid scheme which acts as the centerpiece for this book was an experience shared by tens of thousands of people from all across America. It was a criminal experience and all who participated in it broke the law by committing fraud. As a result, conservative estimates in South Florida alone show that nearly 20,000 people lost $15-20 million.

The perpetrators of this crime were not devious manipulators or felonious underworld types. They were, in fact, well-educated, professional people who were middle-class, law-abiding, taxpaying citizens of good standing. They were also, for the most part, proponents of New Age philosophies. Many, including those who launched this particular fraud, were fervent participants in enlightenment or human potential programs.

During this episode, daughters took funds from mothers, friends from best friends, lovers from each other, executives from secretaries. Each transaction was committed in the name of or justified by some premise of New Age philosophy.

The Airplane Game was written about in *New Age Journal* [21] at the end of 1987 and was dismissed as a heretical and ugly distortion of the New Age teachings. Participants were referred to in this article as greedy and sleazy. The article included a brief, weak explanation of the potential connection of some New Age teachings and the madness that was perpetuated by the Airplane Game. On the whole, the article represented the popular position of

---

[21] *New Age Journal*, November/December, 1987. This article in the largest national publication of its category claimed that 2,000 in Boston's holistic community had participated in the Game, spending more than $2 million. It went on to say that, before Boston, it "was the rage in New York, Philadelphia, Los Angeles, San Francisco."

condemnation which served to officially close the subject of the Airplane Game. No serious inquiry was ever made into how so many people, especially in the New Age community, could have gone so wrong.

However, in New York City, it was a very different story. There the end of the Airplane Game was hysterical, accusatory and litigious. The New York-based, now defunct *Whole Life* magazine with a readership of 250,000 made a crusade of destroying the Game, trying to bring justice to those who were involved. In special editions at the end of 1987 and again in early 1989, the magazine ran lengthy feature stories in which editor and publisher Marc Medoff attacked the Game and its participants with the zeal of a religious reformer. [22]

Medoff, in a special report entitled "The Great Airplane Game Rip-Off, A Shocking Look at the Most Disgraceful Chapter in the History of the New Age Consciousness Movement" wrote, "A community has seemingly gone mad while its leaders have actively engaged in and promoted the madness for personal monetary gain. It is truly a New Age Watergate." One full-page feature listed the names, addresses and phone numbers of thirty-one people the magazine accused of fraud for their participation in the Game. Full page ads offered $1,000 rewards leading to the arrest and conviction of at least three Airplane Game promoters in New York. Thirty-seven people were eventually arrested by New York state authorities in connection with the Airplane Game.

In this outcry, New York was the exception. Perhaps the cause of this debacle was all too clear and far too painful to investigate, fraud and larceny so seemingly impossible to equate with a spiritually-

---

22 *Whole Life's* articles on the Airplane Game were later expanded and reprinted in the book, *Not Necessarily the New Age*, published by Prometheus Books.

minded populace. Yet, clearly this incident was about larceny. And, as with all flimflams, the larceny in the hearts of the criminals is also the very thing that attracts their victims. It is for this reason that many people who lose their money in illegal scams never report such crimes to the police. They know that, rather than having been victimized, they have merely failed in the execution of their own little crime. Professional con artists diabolically understand and exploit this phenomenon. Hence, the abiding and self-justifying aphorism of the con man: You can't cheat an honest man.

Those who plunged like lemmings into the sea of the Airplane Game and the thousands of others who have rushed headlong into scores of MLM programs have all gotten the same message. "Psst, buddy, there's big money in this for you but you need to get in early." What nobody questioned but everyone knew in their hearts was that those behind would surely lose. In fact, as later entrants into the Airplane Game began to voice this reality, those who believed in the Game's infinity were deeply disturbed but not enough so to closely examine what was being said. We didn't want to hear it because, intuitively, we already knew it.

We continued heedlessly to enroll our closest friends and family in the Game all the while wondering if they would be the ones who would enter too late. We hoped not. But if not them, then would it be the families or friends they recruited? Clearly, someone was going to lose. Hopefully, it just wouldn't be us. Indeed, this is the very objective of every con game since time immemorial, beating the system and, yes, at someone else's expense. But isn't that just life with all of its winners and losers? Obviously, the goal is to simply escape being one of the losers.

Even at the pinnacle of the euphoria, when thousands of dollars were literally flowing in all directions, when virtually everyone we knew was joining in the so-called triumph over scarcity, somewhere deep within, we all understood that we were just out to get ours. The fate of others was not our concern as, ultimately, everyone is responsible for themselves. This newfound ideology had lifted us out of victimhood, blame and regret. But, while it had set us free in some sense, it had little to tell us about the management and consequences of our freedom.

Police raided meetings and carried away pilots even as many of us knew that the true perpetration of fraud had occurred within our own minds and hearts. Yet, this incisive fact along with all the righteous condemnations of New Age magazines were deemed irrelevant and immaterial as countless Game players moved directly into further illegal activities such as with Fund America, Inc. Somehow the ripping and tearing at a handful of pilots let everyone else off the hook. It reduced the publicized tirades within the New York New Age community to blind and destructive rationalizations. To escape personal responsibility for participation in the scam even college-educated, privileged and enlightened New Yorkers blithely accepted the label of stupid.

Elsewhere in America, many just took the Fifth as self-incrimination looked far too much like guilt. Yet, even as we experienced an onward and upward moment in time, the truth was undeniable. To round up the lawbreakers in this crime and its aftermath, we had only to look in the mirror.

As to why we committed the crime, there were clues lying about in plain view but, in the mad rush to distance ourselves from public disgrace and humiliation, few of us chose to pick them up and examine them. Interestingly, the est seminar leaders who publicly denied any connection to the Airplane Game and who excoriated its players never questioned how it was that so many of their disciples, citing the seminar's principles and philosophical teachings as justification for participation, had succumbed, en masse, to the Game. There was, in fact, clear refusal in this community to explore any line of inquiry which might have established a philosophical connection between the Game and their seminars.

The result was that *New Age Journal* readers were seldom diverted by advertisements which sounded disturbingly similar to the rhetoric of the Game. Classifieds in this category continued to be read and answered. "Financial Abundance. For complete instructions...Send $3." "Entrepreneurs. Unlimited Income. Six months from now you'll wish you had answered this ad!" Full page ads for positive thinking and motivational audio tapes included offers for *New Age Journal* readers to receive a free preview tape entitled, "The Psychology of Winning." Either as caveat or for comfort, readers were even offered the following: "Becoming a total winner doesn't turn everyone else into losers. On the contrary, total winners help everyone they come in contact with to become winners, too."

Alongside, one could find The Millionaire's Mind Wealth Conditioning Systems, comparing its 12-tape offering to a brain transplant from a self-made millionaire. The cassettes, the ad claimed, "will tattoo the mental conditioning and success traits of a self-made millionaire onto your brain cells." Wow. In another national magazine, a full page ad promised that "In 28 Minutes You'll Be Meditating Like A Zen Monk." In 1989, *Whole Life* magazine offered its own brand of irony, running a 1/3 page ad for a multi-level marketing company in search of "charter leaders interested in a future with BIG REWARDS" on the same page carrying its exposé on New Age greed.

Promises of quick wealth and instant happiness through enrollment permeated New Age literature and programs. No surprise then that when Airplane Game players marched into criminality like crusaders, they held high the banner of New Age philosophy or that few later dared to raise the question of a relationship between New Age beliefs and their behavior.

Greed made us do it, we ultimately realized. Yet, even as we participated in the Game, we had never encountered accusations of greediness. In fact, our life experience reflected the fact that we were no more, no less greedy than most people. So, what did distinguish us from others that we, as a group, fell victim to such a simple-minded swindle while others saw through it and walked away? What, indeed, allowed us to essentially steal from our valued community, to forsake treasured relationships, thus abandoning our prized integrity? And, where on our spiritual journey had we happened onto thinking and beliefs which would, ultimately, support common criminal behavior?

Desperately Seeking Reconciliation

A former pilot strolled along the beach on Singer Island near Palm Beach, taking a day off from his busy professional life. Suddenly he spotted two attractive young women walking in his direction and what would have normally been a pleasurable sight turned to discomfort. Just one year ago, he had enrolled these same two young women in the Airplane Game. Like so many others, they had not achieved pilot status and had, subsequently, lost their $1,500 investments.

Like this pilot who quickly turned away to avoid any possibility of an encounter, many former players found it necessary to follow that same course with people who had been pledged closeness and support. What remained of the now vilified Airplane Game was the discomforting memory of conspiratorial meetings in restaurants and parked cars, of hugs, smiles and promises to share abundance in a never ending cycle of love and prosperity. In the months following the collapse of the Game, most of those who had been involved in such intimate transactions somehow wordlessly agreed to never see each other again. It had simply become more expedient to let the people and the entire affair recede into oblivion.

The awkward, fumbling conversations that might have led to some kind of recovery never took place.

The painful accusations, the disclaimers of responsibility, the acknowledgment of disappointment, the shame and resentment – these honest and potentially healing expressions were never shared. All those pledges of sharing ended with the good times and any money that had been gained seemed, oddly, to have disappeared.

One rationalizing veteran who viewed the Game as a unique course in metaphysical studies printed up and sold tee shirts emblazoned with the words "I Survived the Airplane Game." Seen from the perspective of positioning the Game as a nostalgic, crazy and painful experience, the shirts were intended to provide closure. In fact, not very many sold. Apparently in the end, it was not quite that simple to remove the embarrassment, the arrest records, lost money or friendships.

This lesson-in-life interpretation allowed many to talk in abstract terms about the experience while side-stepping the issues of personal motives and responsibilities. In truth, each of us knew and had always known that the Game was being played out in our own hearts. There had been no overall leader, no judges, no one to enforce the rules. It was equally clear that those who had been apprehended by the authorities and branded leaders were no more culpable than any of the rest of us.

In time, leaders of some of the human potential programs publicly disclaimed any connection with the Game and condemned it for its illegality. Like high priests in a New Age inquisition, they sternly judged the Game's participants, calling them sleaze balls. In fact, participants in the est organization (then called Werner Erhard & Associates) were so heavily involved in the Airplane Game that many est adherents were under the impression that the two were actually related at some official level. In 1987, in order to dispel this notion, an official letter was read to all est seminar participants disclaiming any connection with the Airplane Game.

The aforementioned November 1987 issue of *New Age Journal* carried an extensive piece on the

Game, calling it the soft underbelly of the New Age philosophy. Ram Dass – who himself had naively and enthusiastically played in an earlier scam that also utilized New Age rhetoric – was quoted, urging New Agers to avoid focusing on financial wealth in order to guard against demon greed which pyramid schemes seemed to excite.

Over time, the Game came to be regarded as an aberration, the players labeled heretical and sleazy as the mass phenomenon was officially dismissed. Eventually, through rationalization, avoidance, castigation or secret appreciation, our experiences with the Airplane Game were reconciled and we moved on with our lives. Yet more bitingly than before, we had been left with a longing for the kind of passionate energy which had been felt during the Game's high point. Never before had this need been so clearly revealed as the object of our relentless pursuits through seminars and courses all promising the breakthroughs, insights and peak experiences we hoped would finally assuage our hungering souls. Alas, it was not to be.

Something's Missing

Many New Age followers abandoned traditional religions upon realizing that they frequently tolerated or led to war, racism and social injustice. Likewise, they fled the rigidity, the orthodoxy of unexamined belief systems, the prayers and the rituals. Many were simply disillusioned by the hypocrisy of hierarchies which ignored the flagrant contradictions between the dictates of their dogma and the behaviors of their devotees.

Years later, countless members of this same highly educated, socially conscious, spiritually-principled subculture claimed to have been blithely ignorant of the fraudulent mathematics of pyramid schemes. We were attuned to the rhythms of the Universe yet unable to hear or see the warnings of illegal escapades even when they were emblazoned on newspaper front pages across America. As committed as we were to a better world, we became crassly insensitive to the financial losses of our friends and relatives. We were enlightened with cosmic truths yet suffered no apparent shame from our involvement in a highly publicized scam. Even as we considered ourselves to be continuously self-improving, we had no clue where our beliefs were leading us.

Something was seriously missing from this picture. Perhaps some behaviors could have been attributed to ignorance of the subtleties and extensions of our beliefs. This interpretation carried only so far. There was a driving force beyond the intellectual plane that was short-circuiting connections to conscience and common sense. Looking back, the problem could have been identified as a deep and still unsatisfied spiritual hunger which for each was different yet, for all, sadly reachable only through prosperity. Abundance. Money.

Happiness, it seemed, was somehow beyond us, outside us. It was something to seek, to obtain like another seminar, another breakthrough realization or the financial opportunity of a lifetime. It was never in the present. Whatever we had at any given moment was insufficient. Thus, our behavior as participants of the Airplane Game resembled that of addicts. We neglected jobs and family to frantically, feverishly seek the exhilarating high of pilot status. When we reached it, we wanted more. To get it, we used anyone and everyone. Beyond being greedy and self-centered, we were empty, desolate, desperate and hooked on the belief that an injection of money would fill us up and make us whole persons.[23] Somehow our New Age belief system had

---

[23] Pyramid schemes universally flourish where desperation, spiritual confusion and feelings of insufficiency are rampant. In Romania, where citizens are struggling for survival in an economy ravaged by communism and a maniacal dictator, one seventh of the population
continued on next page

not provided the tools for self-examination which might have addressed this misguided notion.

Ethics essayist Laurence Shames has insightfully noted that the larger American culture itself is based on a kind of infinity game of consumption which advances the notion that there are no limits and that life is fulfilled by acquiring more and more of everything. In *The Hunger for More*, Shames writes, "Consumption kept the workers working, which kept the paychecks coming which kept the people spending, which kept inventors inventing and investors investing, which meant there was more to consume... It was a perfect circle, complete in itself, and empty in the middle."24

So it was with the prosperity-seeking spirituality of the Airplane Game. Along with its legacy of multi-level marketing, it pointed not to a break in the circle but to the emptiness of the middle. Underneath, the players were indistinguishable from the unenlightened. We were all searching for the same things in much the same places. We just used different words to describe our spiritual quest. All of us were equally starved and lost.

Thankfully, as Laurence Shames went on to write in 1991, "There is another way." Shames addressed the narrow and unexamined quest for success in America and the blind homage that is paid to progress. He suggested that each be redefined and

---

invested in a massive pyramid fraud called Caritas. The country's independent newspapers, intellectuals and political opposition leaders all sounded the alarm that Caritas was a classic pyramid scheme and would collapse with millions of Romanians losing their last remaining savings. "Ubi Caritas," Charles Lane, *The New Republic*, November 8, 1993, pp. 9-10.

24 Laurence Shames, *The Hunger for More*. New York: Vintage Books, 1991. The premise of this book is that on Black Monday, October 19, 1987, when the stock market lost 23% of its total value, a pivotal moment occurred in U.S. history in which ethics and values were laid bare compelling many in the 'me-generation' to re-examine their lifestyles, goals and values.

that we focus on "success in service, success in originality, success even in contentment.... Progress could be measured in terms of equity or social calm rather than just growth. The great moral and also imaginative challenge now facing us is to begin to cultivate a sense of purpose that has less to do with more and more to do with better."

Many years have passed and the Airplane Game is dead and mostly forgotten. So, why delve into this old story? Why rub the wounds of a forgotten mistake? For one main reason. A truism in the world of flimflam is that a person who is swindled once is extremely vulnerable to being fleeced again and again as witnessed by the countless variations on the Airplane Game that continue to crop up among these very same ranks.

Notable among these new outcroppings was the Friends Gifting Network which offered the familiar $1,500 membership with a return of $12,000 for those who got in early. Hundreds of people from the New Age community were involved and millions of dollars were offered up. Promoters and participants claimed the Gifting Network was a legal and ethical multi-level marketing company. However, a quick scan via modem of newspapers around the country revealed that the Gifting Network had already been exposed and prosecuted in cities around the nation.[25]

Periodically, appearing under new names then running their brief and inevitable course, these schemes now emerge bearing the more respectable,

---

[25] "An illegal pyramid scam being marketed to suburban police officers, among others, is spreading in Philadelphia and its suburbs," officials said yesterday. Thus Attorney General Ernie Preate Jr. warned consumers against participating in the so-called Friends Network Gifting Program, a pyramid scam that promised 700 percent profits, tax free. Preate said lawyers from his Bureau of Consumer Protection office in Philadelphia are holding hearings beginning today with 23 individuals who allegedly participated in the scheme." Frederick Cusic, *Philadelphia Inquirer*, July 13, 1994, page B-3.

legal veneer of multi-level marketing while leading ever increasing numbers of people down the same dead end. If the dissection of the Airplane Game experience can result in a heightened awareness and, thus, closer examination of one of today's most insidious business trends, the examination, however painful, can be counted as highly worthwhile.

Déja Vu

About six months of silence fell upon the participating network after the Airplane Game was crushed. Reconciliations took time and friendships shifted. Along the way beliefs were modified, judgments were rendered and events were re-interpreted.

Soon, however, the phones began ringing again as hope and salvation for many had been renewed, this time through a legal system which promised to be as lucrative as the Airplane Game. It was called multi-level or network marketing. In South Florida, many of the earliest and most ardent champions of MLM emerged from the ranks of veteran Airplane Game pilots. In fact, several who had made tens of thousands from the Game have since gone on to make hundreds of thousands as up-line distributors for one of various network marketing companies.

It was about this time that the worlds of MLM and New Age began to merge in South Florida and across the country. One of the first MLM organizations to arrive on the scene after the Airplane Game debacle was NSA, a producer of home water purifiers. Designed to filter water through charcoal – which only removed chlorine – the NSA product was, nonetheless, guaranteed to protect our bodies from invisible cancer-causing poisons in our drinking water. Next, Nu Skin burst upon the scene as a supplier of skin and hair products which promised to forestall the aging process. Along the way and perhaps in response to these new MLM entrants, Amway, having expanded its product line to include almost any kind of consumable item, made a strong resurgence among previously skeptical New Agers.

Then in 1990, an organization that promised to clearly outstrip the most aggressive of the multi-levels already flourishing in the state arrived in Florida. It was called Fund America, Inc. Established in California, Fund America had already generated ecstatic reports from participants and some business analysts even as an October 1989 cover article in the Orange County, California, business magazine, *Metropolitan Journal,* ran a story on Fund America entitled "PYRAMID POWER." Reprints of this article highlighting the same type of beaming countenances that had been worn by Airplane Game inauguration witnesses just a year before were included in the Fund America marketing packages which were given to new sales representatives.

In this case, however, the dollars had escalated. One featured sales representative for Fund America reported a $12,000 income per month resulting from his 10,000-member sales network. The article went on to report that the company expected sales to reach one billion dollars in several years according to the Fund America president.

A side bar article carried a revealing description of a Fund America recruitment meeting which had been attended by mostly white collar workers under the age of 50. According to the article, the common attitude among the attendees, was "one of hope, even desperation, which says, 'I've worked my butt off for other people all my life and I've never been paid what I'm worth. This is my chance to get rich, to get what I deserve.'"

The speakers at the recruitment meeting announced to the expectant audience that they were "gonna learn about the most incredible business opportunity you've ever seen." The first speaker explained that under this system, one could save while spending, even spend your way into retirement. All that was required to get in on the bonanza was a $140 membership fee which allowed members of Fund America to take advantage of rebates the company had negotiated with major corporations for purchases of many items people were already buying including long distance phone and travel agency services.

Products and services made available under the Fund America rebate system included Hertz Rental

Car, Ask-Mr.-Foster Travel service, Tele-Bouquet Service, a Master Card credit card and a large consumer catalogue for mail order purchases of thousands of name brand products. Actual prices on most items were no better than discounts that were widely available. But, the inspiring appeal of this program was that one could gain an override on the purchases of thousands of other people's purchases with no effort whatsoever except to achieve their initial enrollment. [26]

Members could accrue rebates on their own purchases and, subsequently, receive a percentage of the purchases of customers and distributors they recruited which, in theory, actually meant making money in this network by spending money. Additionally, rebates could automatically be placed in a company savings account which would further compound the member's earnings.

Fund America's founder said he was inspired to create the system upon observing that Americans were not saving, taking the position that he was transforming consumerism into painless frugality. No behavior change was required, he claimed. One need only enroll in the system. As the Fund America literature stated, "Our program is geared for the individual who lives for today, knows that planning for the future and retirement is important, but doesn't want to sacrifice now to do it." Abundance, once again, required no struggle, just participation.

Reminiscent of the pilot, co-pilot, crew and passenger system with which thousands of Airplane game participants were so familiar, Fund America organized its players as representatives, associates, managers, directors, executive directors and presidential directors. "An independent

---

[26] As depicted in a Fund America marketing bulletin, this typical compensation potential for a single individual required five groups delivering a total volume of 100 memberships per month, in other word, a network downline of 6,000 people.

representative may sponsor other people to be independent representatives. Those independent representatives sponsored by an independent representative may also sponsor independent representatives," the company brochure stated. As a Fund America agent, the more you invested, initially, the further up the commission chain you placed yourself, the bigger your cut would be from those you and others enrolled into the buying network.

The roll out of Fund America, Inc. in Florida set the phone lines on fire. Several former seminar devotees who had moved to California and joined the exploding growth of Fund America in that state boarded planes and flew immediately back to Florida for its premiere. Old friendships and neglected family contacts were re-established, all followed by the inevitable invitation to partake in a magnificent new opportunity. Mass meetings were held and the old spirit of the Airplane Game had returned. In grandiose language equivalent to the cosmic claims of the Airplane Game, the Fund America brochures stated, "Network marketing could quite possibly be the ideal business evolving over years to become one of the most effective, powerful marketing systems in the world."

Then, like a recurring nightmare, the police suddenly intervened. The president of Fund America was arrested for fraud in Rhode Island and the State of Florida began aggressively prosecuting the company. That dreaded term, pyramid scheme, was emblazoned in front of Fund America followers. Newspapers reported that millions of dollars had been bilked from victims.[27] Many who had joined Fund America in Florida and, subsequently, lost their money as it collapsed in disgrace were the very same people who had entered and lost in the Airplane Game several years prior. As if in perfect

---

[27] *Sun-Sentinel*, July 20, 1990, Fort Lauderdale, Florida, page 3B.

symmetry, those who made thousands of fast dollars in Fund America were among the ones who had done similarly in the Airplane Game.

Television news reports showed the leather-bound Fund America distributor kits like props in a flimflam operation and told how the company lured unsuspecting members into the purchase of distributorships for thousands of dollars. The typical initial investment was $3,200. A Florida state prosecutor described Fund America as slick, utilizing a seductive sales presentation. "It appeals to the weakness we all have to be rich," he said. "A classic pyramid scheme," an investigator for the Florida comptroller's office called it. "The people at the top make a lot of money," he said, "but those later on..."

State officials estimated that Fund America had earned more than $8 million in South Florida alone in about 100 days. According to state officials quoted in one newspaper account, the president of Fund America faced another arrest warrant in England for conspiracy to defraud based on an earlier pyramid scheme. Authorities advised the shocked and disappointed supporters of Fund America not to expect a return of any monies.

Although Fund America was declared illegal by the authorities, the police did not pursue or arrest any Florida distributors, many of whom were fervent New Age believers and Airplane Game veterans. This time, a true ring leader had been identified leaving everyone else, even those who profited enormously, in a position to safely claim victim status.

False Profits

Section III
Kissing Cousins: MLM and Pyramid Schemes

The Fountain of Youth Revisited

The scene is now becoming typical. They do not know each other and yet a friendly familiarity pervades the hotel conference room which is nearly filled to its capacity of 500. Like members of a secret lodge, people signal each other with ritual smiles and white collar graces. They are wearing the stylish uniforms of the upwardly mobile or, at least, upwardly aspiring. There are no cut-off jeans, sweatshirts, labor union jackets or caps, no work boots among them. These enrollees are from the managerial and sales classes of America, the domain where potential prevails over actuality, where what you want to be counts for more than what you presently are.

As yesterday's sales are already history, attention is now riveted upon tomorrow's possibilities. Attained positions on the corporate ladder are mere stepping stones and job satisfaction means career death. It is clear that everyone is always selling and, therefore, all in attendance are girded with outward self-confidence. They are aware that personal presentation and a carefully molded self, ultimately, determine the outcome of all transactions. Yet for all the right thinking, expensive haircuts and fashionable clothing, a scent of nervous anxiety is exuded which is stronger than any designer cologne.

On this special evening, these people have come to hear about an extraordinary opportunity. Anticipation and keen interest are further energized by a sense of urgency. Everyone there acknowledges that extraordinary opportunities come only rarely. Timing is critical.

Nobody present knows this company but the name, Nu Skin, sparks interest as many in attendance at this function would love to shed old skins weathered by failures and disappointments for new. Here might be the answer to the longing for renewed, youthful exuberance and a real chance for the luxuriant life promised along with much more by the Nu Skin products and promotion.

If one has doubts, the company offers tapes with inaudible, subliminal messages that can be used to retrain that stubborn subconscious which for years has been subverting success. The all-natural products, the ingenious sales program, the Nu Skin promotional video claims, are all bulletproof. The baby-boomer market, it says, refuses to age and is starving for these products. That's why Nu Skin offers lotions to rejuvenate those furrowed brows, tonics to address receding hair lines and cover thinning crowns, weight loss formulas to restore youthful figures and shampoos to return luster to permed, colored and graying heads of hair.

On the stage at the front of the room, a chart graphically displays how enrollees can exponentially compound their own energies and time. Here is the answer to prayers of quiet desperation. For in their quest for the Holy Grail of success, many, including those in their 20's, believe that they have reached the limits of their personal resources of time and effort. Unemployment has ravaged their circles of friends. They are mortgaged up to their necks and few have any savings at all. A profound insecurity has come to grip their psyches as they walk past homeless people on the streets every day. A month or two without income and they, too, could be on the streets.

This vague fear of having exhausted all finite resources for success conflicts disturbingly with the desirable image of being the no-limit person Wayne Dyer describes, a winner with unlimited power. After all, success is primarily a matter of positive mental attitude, of creating a vision of success and of training the subconscious through affirmations. Just listen to the tapes or read the personal development books of Napoleon Hill, Robert Schuller, Zig Ziglar and Tony Robbins.

The message at this meeting is how time and energy can be exponentially increased, not by more hard work, but through a dramatic breakthrough in capitalism called multi-level marketing. It is sweeping the marketplace and, in a few short years, the majority of all goods will be delivered to the consumer in this manner. The real miracle of this business breakthrough is that it will eventuate in the redistribution of the wealth which has previously been concentrated in the hands of advertisers and numerous levels of wholesalers and retailers. MLM simply eliminates all unnecessary functionaries in the sales and marketing process and redistributes freed up monies to participants in the marketing network. The Nu Skin message is that retailing is dying, that the new order of business resides in the non-bureaucratic network in which everyone will sell to one another in endless and effortless chains.

Another view of the same promise was offered in a May 1990 commentary by the editor of *Success* magazine. In his recounting of the possible future MLM offers as it permeates our economy, he described a family dinner table at which everyone is selling something to everyone else. Mom confers with Dad about the water filters she represents. Dad, in turn, invites her to a recruitment meeting for a great opportunity he is promoting. Junior is listening to a motivational tape that he purchased from his upline distributor which exhorts him to meet his monthly sales quota. Even the family's three-year-old is selling a magazine subscription to her Granddad. Network marketing, the article predicts, will fuse Americans from coast to coast into one "gigantic, pulsating sales ameba."

According to Nu Skin, one has only to look at the chart which reveals that any network member can compound his or her earnings explosively by producing just five layers of downliners. In addition, these earnings will continue to accrue forever, making the idea of savings obsolete. Hard work has been rendered an archaic and self-limiting way of life. Networking can make financial freedom available to everyone. All you have to do is enroll.

For an hour and a half, people listen to the success stories of Nu Skin distributors. Some are meek and grateful for their good fortune. They want it for their audience, too. They say that if they can do it, anyone can. Others boast of their wealth, taunting their listeners to give up whatever they are doing unless it can offer the same financial opportunities they have realized as Nu Skin distributors. Unheard of incomes of $10,000 and $50,000 per month are casually and confidently reported.

"I know about those of you with jobs," says one successful upliner. "J.O.B., Journey Of the Broke!" Professions, trades and artistic pursuits are similarly derided. One of the speakers identifies himself as a former rabbi. "Would I have given up a $90,000 a year religious job if this were not an opportunity of a lifetime?" he asks.

Some speakers berate and others mock. Some exalt the audience for its potential while portraying a sensuous, luxuriant image of what lies ahead upon joining the network. The best of the world is offered – beautiful homes, expensive jewelry, fashionable clothing, freedom and the time to take vacations to exotic locations.

The speakers reiterate that it is the MLM system which has enfolded them in the security and pleasures of six-figure incomes, not any special talents or efforts of their own. The enrollment of downline organizations is depicted as a kind of benevolent missionary work which is simply about spreading the word of MLM and its amazing benefits. Who wouldn't want to offer this to their family and all their closest friends?

Now all those mind-training tapes and positive mental attitudes are beginning to pay off and people are becoming mesmerized and passionately aroused by visions of six-figure incomes, comfortable, worry-free retirements and a sense of belonging to an army of well-dressed, positive thinking winners. Success, oh, sweet success. Surely this time it has arrived! Everyone in attendance knows this message is true because each is desperately wanting what is promised. Sales are skyrocketing, the speaker claims ecstatically. The company is in momentum. The Nu

Skin train to financial independence is leaving tonight. What are you all waiting for?

False Profits

Family, Friendships and the Professions in the MLM World

*The bargaining manner, the
huckstering animus, the
memorized theology of pep, the
commercialized evaluation of
personal traits – they are all
around us; in public and in
private there is the tang and
feel of salesmanship.*[28]

– *C. Wright Mills*

...The room was dimly lit, cool and serene. Enjoying the appropriate sense of vulnerability which accompanies bodywork with a trusted therapist, the patient was fully relaxed in preparation for a restorative massage. The masseur whom the patient had regularly visited for several years knocked gently on the door to see if his client was ready for treatment.

As was their custom, the first few moments of the hour-long massage were spent in friendly exchange, usually chat about healing or spiritual matters which mutually interested them. On this day, the masseur was especially talkative as he and his new girlfriend had recently taken up residence together and he was excited about the changes in his life.

---

[28] Sociologist C. Wright Mills thus described the growing influence of direct sales in our society, relating this increasing sales influence to the over-capacity of the post World War II economy in which industry was no longer affordably meeting consumer demand. Therefore, new demand had to be created, he said. Written in the early 1950's before multi-level marketing had even gained a foothold, Mills' insightful impressions are now understated as today's MLMs also feed upon the growing economic insecurity, unemployment and underemployment that characterize the economy of the 80's and 90's. C. Wright Mills, *White Collar*. New York: Oxford University Press, 1953, pp. 161.

After sharing a few details of his move, the masseur suddenly and eagerly began talking about a company offering nutritional products that his girlfriend had become involved with some months earlier. While the topic of nutrition was not an uncommon one, the way the masseur was introducing it somehow caused the client to feel a breach in the normally trusting atmosphere of the treatment room. A sense of tension or the presence of some pressure had intruded. The masseur's words seemed so familiar – it's a great opportunity, everybody we know is getting involved with the company and nobody has to sell anything. Then, there it was – the fact that not only had the masseur moved in with his girlfriend but they were also now in business together. And, the new hot topic was an extraordinary line of herbal products that he wanted all his friends and clients to know about.

As a business person, the client had already heard plenty of these pitches and she was clearly not interested. But because she had been coming to this masseur for several years and believed that she had a special relationship with him, she felt free to honestly tell him that she was happy for him but was not personally interested in this kind of opportunity.

In the same way that she felt the tension arrive in the room, the client now suddenly experienced an equally clear presence of – not disappointment – but disapproval. Had her eyes been open, she might have seen her masseur frown, thinking about how foolish her lack of interest was. The normal time for their chat period had been extended for this discussion but now it was time for quiet. Except now, instead of the gentle, caring silence that this client had come to expect as the accompaniment to her massage, there was a new air of efficiency, a feeling that the masseur just wanted to get this hour over with, perhaps, so that he could move on to his next client. Maybe the next one would be smarter, would actually understand the wonderful opportunity he was offering to all his special clients.[29]

...At a small outdoor cafe, a couple met a young woman who they knew and admired for her work as the program director for a prominent philanthropic organization. As the couple had heard of her resignation from this modestly paid social action job, they inquired as to her current employment and her general well-being.

With barely a response to either inquiry, the young woman began telling the couple about a remarkable new product that she was representing through its only source of distribution which was a network marketing company. She went on to position this secret amalgam of herbs and vitamins as having miraculous properties, even producing excellent results for cancer patients and AIDS sufferers. In fact, she claimed, other chronic and diverse conditions such as acne, allergies, constipation and arthritis were easily remedied with this herbal elixir.

Without regard for the dubious nature of her claims, she clearly expected the same kind of respect and seriousness in response to this pitch that her social issues presentations had prior earned. In fact,

---

[29] In addition to dentists, chiropractors and all kinds of wellness community practitioners, the medical profession is becoming firmly entrenched in MLM. Physicians are now being encouraged to use their esteemed positions of trust as leverage in the presentation and sale of healthcare products strictly for financial gain. In an excerpt from the September, 1995 issue of *Physician's Management*, an article entitled "The Physician as Entrepreneur," doctors were urged to turn to network marketing as a way of offsetting possible reduced earnings from patient billings which might result from changes in the insurance arena. With regard to the opportunities for physicians to flourish financially through the sale of nutritional products, the article states, "As a physician, you are in a unique position to take advantage of network marketing... First of all, you start out in a position of respect. Patients generally will do what their physicians recommend, and this is especially the case when it comes to supplements."

she hardly seemed to notice the level of difference between her former efforts which were directed at reducing human suffering and the business deal she was now peddling. Thus, she sailed on in her pitch to these friends telling them that news of this miracle cure would not be available through press conferences or medical journals but only at roll-out meetings like the one she was on her way to in another Florida city.

Here she dropped an authoritative reference to the six-figure earnings of some of the distributors, casually airing the news that she, herself, had every reason to expect to earn more than a million dollars over the next two years. Pausing to allow these extraordinary income figures to make their intended impression, she next asked the couple to attend a local meeting so they, too, could hear more about this extraordinary opportunity.

Upon their decline, the young woman arrogantly switched her attention to the financial limitations of the work that each of these people was currently doing. In stunned silence, the couple listened as this former humanitarian and social servant revealed a new, singular and embarrassingly intense interest in raw commercial concerns. Only out of respect for their past association were they able to refrain from calling into question her credibility. Abruptly, this time of discomfort ended as the young woman rushed off to her roll-out meeting.

...A teacher and seminar leader whose healing and compassionate work had touched and benefited hundreds in the South Florida New Age community called one of her earliest followers to report her excitement about an MLM company she had learned about. The company was marketing a line of herbal-based cosmetics.

Describing the products with a very out-of-character reference to "top-drawer," this new MLM recruit claimed to be seeking evaluation of the product and the company's operations. Before her student could alert his former teacher to all the industry hazards he is aware of as a result of countless solicitations from other friends, the teacher plunged ahead, excitedly discussing the huge downline organization she believed would be available to her through teaching network.

In fact, she was quick to point out that this student and his wife could, similarly, find themselves at the top of a very successful downline by utilizing all their contacts. Brushing aside any raised questions regarding the probabilities of success for those clients and friends who might find themselves on such a downline, the teacher doggedly focused on the immediate financial opportunity.

"This may be the Universe's way of letting you become free to write and travel and do whatever else you want to do," she suggested bringing to the fore not only her well-known counseling style but her privileged knowledge of his privately-held desires. Thus taking advantage of the trust and intimacy that had become a part of their counseling relationship, this once-revered teacher was soliciting her network of clients in an effort to entice them to join her in an allegedly wealth-producing MLM scheme. The promise of all that money had instantly turned this spiritual teacher into the self-appointed head of her own aggressive sales organization.

...On a scheduled business trip to Chicago, a business traveler arranged to have dinner with an acquaintance who lived in that city. While they had not met before in person, the two men were linked by work they had both done for a national anti-hunger organization and the shared personal concerns that this commitment had represented.

An enjoyable evening over dinner was anticipated as both a break from work and an opportunity to develop a new friendship. The traveler noted that while he had put aside all thoughts of business for the evening, his new friend came accompanied by his briefcase.

Halfway through dinner, the purpose of the briefcase was made clear and, with the revelation of all its Nu Skin contents, the tone of the evening changed dramatically. All talk of continued work on hunger prevention campaigns was swept away as this MLMer suddenly became electrified by talk of Nu Skin income potential. The trust and relatedness that had begun to grow between these two men paled in importance as the new priority for this meeting emerged.

Cleverly manipulating the evening's conversation to reflect Nu Skin's party line, the MLMer began a full court press to enroll his new friend suggesting that this opportunity would change his life for the better. It was, in fact, offered as the answer to all the myriad life dilemmas the two had been pondering philosophically over dinner.

Plowing on without concern for his dinner partner's lack of response, the new friend informed the traveler that he felt compelled to share the fact that they could both look forward to enjoying this incredible financial future through Nu Skin. To underscore his intended largesse, the MLMer began jotting down numbers on his napkin showing the exponential growth of his income, based upon enrollments of a 1,000-person downline.

Neither the rebuttals, resistance nor the now-obvious distaste for this blatant sales pitch registered on the MLMer. Even as the evening took on an awkward embarrassment, it was impossible to stop the solicitation. In place of the anticipated evening of shared pleasantries, our business traveler felt lured, then snared into listening to an insensitive and self-centered pitch to which he would never having, knowingly, exposed himself.

...In another city, a young entrepreneur, part-owner of a new but growing publishing company which was experiencing typical new business cash flow problems noticed that his brother-in-law, a recent Amway enrollee, had begun taking a strange new interest in the young man's marriage. Keenly interested in the family's finances, the brother-in-law expressed concern over his sister's leaving their two-year-old in daycare to take a job which, while furthering her own career, was primarily to support the family during lean months.

A luncheon invitation materialized and the brother-in-law used the opportunity to urge his sister's husband to join his downline of Amway reps. The target of this pitch clearly indicated that he did not want to mix business with family only to hear his brother-in-law treat his objections as irresponsible in light of the potential income he was offering.

Circumventing the young man's lack of interest and refusal to accept further luncheon invitations, the brother-in-law turned his attention back to his sister. If she were an Amway rep, he insisted, she would not have to be working outside of her home with their child in a daycare center. He blatantly discredited her husband for his refusal to seize the Amway opportunity while persisting in a business that was not fully supporting his family. Couldn't she see that Amway presented the answer to their income needs along with the way to achieve a proper family life?

...Elsewhere the faithful and hundreds of new hopefuls clapped, cheered and listened intently to a persuasive, uplifting, challenging and inspirational presentation offered by the representative of yet another MLM organization. The meeting was a regular event designed to support current representatives in their enrollment efforts with potential initiates.

After the meeting, distributors huddled with their invited friends and relatives. A young woman manager of a local office for temporary employees earnestly explained to her cluster that she, personally, was building a downline organization of 1,000 distributors from whom she would receive overrides. She explained that it would take about that many sub-distributors in order for her to achieve her personal goal of earning more than $100,000 a year.

One friend asked how she could recruit so many distributors. She answered that the number was not large at all in consideration of the fact that this same opportunity to easily earn $100,000 would be available to all those she enlisted. That extraordinary possibility alone would attract and motivate countless people. Each could then build a 1,000-person downline organization of their own. In effect, she concluded, her downline would be built by other people all seeking the same goal. "It is the wave of the future," she explained.

Her friend pointed out that, if all her downliners achieved their goal, there would be one million distributors in their area. Could the area possibly support that many? Another listener pointed out that there were 500 people at this one night's rally, most of them current distributors. Did that mean that all of these people were also trying to build 1,000-member distribution organizations? And, were they all promising their downliners the chance to earn $100,000 a year by enrolling a 1,000-person downline team?

That would explain what all the excitement was about. Surely people wouldn't get so enthusiastic over earning just a little extra money each month from selling products to family and friends. Nor could the products themselves create such eagerness. That must be it! They're all seeking the same goal – 1,000-member downlines which would lead to those six-figure incomes.

Another in the group who had been listening to these questions pointed out that, if all those people were actually working on building downlines, then millions of enrollees would be needed to fulfill their dreams in just this one small area of South Florida.

A bit irritated at the apparent slowness of her group or perhaps disappointed in their lack of ambition, the young woman shifted her tone. Looking about to be sure that no one beyond her circle of friends and relatives can hear her, she confided that very few of the hopefuls would ever really succeed. "Most are losers," she revealed. "It's a kind of numbers game," she confided. The pitch was that you just have to keep enrolling people until you find winners. Even some of the losers you enroll will enroll others and your hottest downliners might come from such a source. But, when you do get enough winners on your team, your future is assured. "Since so many will fail," she said, "the territory would never be over-saturated with representatives. The opportunity would always be there for anyone making the investment."

Myriad questions entered the minds of several of the listeners but, since they were friends, they did not pose them that evening. Yet, lingering in their minds, was one very troubling thought. While they had attended the evening out of caring or respect, they wondered at having been told, in not so many words, that the only interest their friend now had in them was related to their becoming part of her new downline. And, it didn't really seem to matter to her whether they, eventually, were winners or losers in this new game.

Yes, But This One's Legal!

While there are legal distinctions which separate the Airplane Game from the typical multi-level marketing operation, the spirit that energizes, the rhetoric which supports and the value system underpinning MLM companies are the same factors that create the foundation for pyramid schemes. Despite personal denials and rationalizations by many participants, the question of legality of the Airplane Game was settled and enforced. The Game was a classic fraud and was declared so by state authorities around the country. The legality of specific MLM companies, as the Fund America case illustrated, is not as clear.

Although MLM promoters often say this is a radical new form of capitalism, in fact, it is a matured concept that is in the midst of resurgence. Most analysts attribute this comeback not to the system's success for distributors but rather to the rise in unemployment and the new insecurity within established corporations caused by downsizing and restructuring. The growth of state lotteries which economists also attribute to rising economic insecurity corresponds to the growth of MLMs in recent years.

Established in 1945, Nutrilite, an operation which set up a multi-level commission program to pay for sales of nutritional supplements, is believed to have been the very first MLM company. Amway and Shaklee have been around since the mid 1950's and, interestingly, the two founders of Amway, Richard DeVos and Jay Van Andel, worked for Nutrilite.

Recently, MLM has begun to attract companies formerly based on hit-the-street, door-to-door selling. Fuller Brush company, for example, a household name in the 50's for door-to-door sales, fell on hard times with its market share dropping below 1%. Now the company is shifting its compensation plan to MLM, offering its 12,000 reps the chance to recruit other reps and earn commissions on top of their sales. The company says it hopes to soon grow its sales force to 100,000.

The total MLM industry is estimated at between 5 and 10 million distributors who sell between $10- and $20-billion of goods. That turns out to be about $2,000 of gross sales per distributor per year, leaving a profit of less than $50 a month on average. While people in the industry itself estimate that 90-95% of all MLM companies go out of business within a couple of years, the actual number may be much higher. In light of this assumption and with the knowledge that it is the earliest distributors at the top who make a lot of money very fast, a subsequent MLM bankruptcy could wind up being an enormous financial success for the founders.

As writer David Owen stated in the *Atlantic Monthly*, "MLM is alluring because it seems to offer not a job but a means of transcending the laws of economics. But the appeal is an illusion. Those tantalizing compensation schedules actually work against the average distributor whose sales efforts serve mostly to line the pockets of other people." [30]

Cosmetic companies, producers of holistic diet drinks, distributors of vitamins and a wide variety of other consumer items with built-in repeatable business have made their dramatic debuts and vigorously recruited among the ranks of former Airplane Game enthusiasts. Each of these dynamic new programs is based on the development of an endless chain of hierarchically-connected distributors, identical to that which linked Airplane Game participants to infinity. Likewise, each recruit to these MLMs is presented with the same breathtaking possibility of building a small army of downline distributors on whose labor they can live luxuriously, forever.

---

30 David Owen, "Dreams and Downlines." *Atlantic Monthly*, October, 1987, pp. 84-90.

From inception; network marketing companies have skirted state lottery laws by basing promises of profits on product sales rather than the enrollment fees of new distributors. Even so, this line of legality is very fine and many such companies have over recent years been investigated and/or prosecuted. For example, the January 3, 1992 edition of the *Wall Street Journal* reported that Nu Skin had entered into agreements with prosecutors in Ohio, Michigan, Illinois, Florida and Pennsylvania to change its sales practices after investigators had charged the firm with operating a pyramid scheme.

According to an article in the *Boston Globe*, the same day that Nu Skin settled its case with the five states, "Connecticut filed suit against Nu Skin International, charging the company with operating a pyramid scheme in its product distribution. The lawsuit, filed in Hartford Superior Court, charges the company with misleading potential distributors about the money they could make." In its settlement with the other states, Nu Skin admitted no wrongdoing but did agree to give 90 percent refunds on unsold goods to distributors who chose to drop out. The company also said it would pay the states to cover the costs of their investigations.

Like some of the other early MLMs, Herbalife was charged by state officials with running an illegal pyramid scheme. A 1993 *Forbes* magazine article on Herbalife broadly classified the company as a pyramid. By the definition used in the *Forbes* article, "Pyramid refers to the sales organization which is multi-layered with each layer recruiting a larger number of sales people who in turn recruit another level."

Those who rushed from the Airplane Game directly to MLM knew from experience that the power and magic resided in the recruitment potential of one's own sales organization rather than in product sales. Few could say they were truly excited by water filters, cosmetics, skin lotions or laundry soap. The real attraction was to be found in the mystical mathematics of pyramids.

All you have to do is find five distributors. Then they each find five distributors and they in turn each find five and then they find five. See? Now you have over 600 agents working for you. If each sells just $350 a month of product and you receive only a 5% override on their sales, you have a guaranteed monthly income of more than $10,000!

No mention is made of the mathematical progression beyond the first four or five levels. Yet, if the formula is followed out to just a few more levels on the five-get-five premise, the numbers quickly move into the millions. In like fashion, the mathematical chances of success for the downliners are also not closely analyzed. Often enrollees are not given any idea where on the chain they are entering the system. Nonetheless, it is understood that the earlier you get on board, the better. Many of those who had played the Airplane Game understood this fact better than others and so were among the first to gain strategic top positions in some MLM organizations.[31]

In an August 3, 1992 interview, financial investigator for the Consumer Litigation Section of the Florida Department of Legal Affairs, Jim Lyons, summed up the legal issues plaguing many MLM companies as "lyin', cheatin', and stealin'."[32] He said

---

31 The pyramid structure of the Airplane Game was the source of wealth for those getting in early yet losses incurred by thousands who entered late were also mathematically inevitable. Likewise with MLMs, the potential for the growth of the organization offers extraordinary income potential but the same mathematical principle ensures that most will fail. In other words, the success of a few is based upon the failure of many.

32 The "lyin', cheatin' and stealin'" that Lyons said he had commonly encountered included front loading new distributors with large amounts of inventory, wildly exaggerated claims of income potential, failure to inform new distributors of the number of competitive distributors in a territory and allowing unlimited numbers of distributors in any area. He also encountered an abusive practice of
continued on next page

his own department's focus was not on the illegal pyramid aspects of MLMs but rather on whether or not they engage in unfair business practices and misrepresent themselves. Indeed, he had found the industry rife with misrepresentation.

Florida has, subsequently, enacted legislation specifically to control the growing abuses of MLMs. The new rules require that firms disclose how many distributors have joined their companies and how many have attained publicized income levels. Additionally, at least 51% of any such company's income must be derived from product sales rather than from distributor or marketing fees charged to new recruits.

Lyons went on to personally dispute the two most common claims of MLM companies which undergird their persuasive enrollments: that MLM is the wave of the future, destined to surpass retail as the prime method of product distribution; and, that MLM is a more cost effective method of delivering products to consumers. He found no evidence that MLM would work for most products. In fact, with sometimes up to seven layers of distributor overrides plus the parent company's profit taking, Lyons pointed out that many MLM products are anything but cost effective. Rather than for any new value they offer, Lyons noted that most MLM companies sell unregulated products that do not require high manufacturing costs. Finally, he said that he personally attributes the extraordinary growth of MLM to the increasing levels of greed in our culture and to the high unemployment rates that threaten financial security.

In an August 25, 1992 interview David Augland, Chief Assistant Statewide Prosecutor in Florida, said he finds no structural difference between classic

---

requiring monthly minimum orders that are obtained by holding the new distributor's credit card number for automatic monthly billing.

pyramid organizations[33] and most network marketing companies. Augland's office prosecuted Fund America, Inc. and went on to investigate several of the largest multi-level marketing companies in Florida.

After attending many multi-level marketing rallies and sales meetings, Augland has said that he is personally fascinated by the phenomenon of glazed eyes and emotional frenzy generated at such meetings, noting their striking resemblance to cults. He said the extraordinary growth of multi-level marketing companies, in his view, represents the democratization of greed which has objectified all relationships. Augland said he sees the abuse of

---

[33] Pyramids are commonly called Ponzi schemes referring to the 1920's Boston con man, Charles A. Ponzi. When Ponzi promised investors a 50 percent return in 45 days, customers swarmed his office to get in on the anticipated bonanza. Euphoria swept the financial community. The plan lasted about eight months before the inevitable crash with losses mounting to between $15 million and $20 million. The later hopefuls, numbering in the thousands, lost everything. It was soon realized that Ponzi was paying off the first group of investors with funds from the next group of investors. He had no wondrous business enterprise or any secret knowledge of economics that was generating these great profits. He was simply using the investors' own money to create the illusion of an extraordinary business breakthrough. The real source of the godsend was the investors themselves.

Ponzi did five years in prison but soon after his release was arrested for a land fraud in Florida. Eventually, he was deported to his native Italy and later went to Brazil to represent an Italian airline in that country. Ponzi finally died a pauper in a charity ward in Rio De Janeiro. His name lives on as a reference to all robbing-Peter-to-pay-Paul or pyramid schemes around the world.

Author Nicole Biggart, in her sociological study of MLMs, speculates that the legacy of Ponzi may have inspired the formation of multi-level distribution companies. She does establish a connection between MLMs and a practice started in the late 20's of paying finder's fees to distributors for locating new salespersons. Nicole Woolsey Biggart, *Charismatic Capitalism*. Chicago: The University of Chicago Press, 1989, pp. 44-46.

people's trust in multi-level frauds as just as violent and intrusive as normal crimes.

Waving the banner of legality, the resemblance of MLM to the embarrassing incident of crime and craziness of the Airplane Game is seldom noticed. In fact, MLM solicitations have become so much a part of our daily lives, our very community that people rarely stop to consider their meaning even as the striking similarity between the two phenomena lies nakedly on the surface.

A notable example of public deception in the MLM world came to light in the world-famous O. J. Simpson murder case. Simpson's attorneys told the jurors that he suffered from chronic rheumatoid arthritis which rendered him physically incapable of murdering his wife, Nicole, and her friend, Ron Goldman. Simpson showed the jurors the swollen joints of his knees as proof. However, prosecutors uncovered video tapes that had been produced just three months prior in which Simpson proclaimed that his arthritis had almost disappeared. On tape, he had attributed his remarkable medical recovery to a food supplement drink called Juice Plus which was sold through the multi-level marketing company, NSA. Simpson was the international spokesman and promoter of this product and his statements about the miraculous healing abilities of Juice Plus had been made at a rally to recruit NSA distributors.

In another case in point, televangelist and right-wing politician, Pat Robertson, of the 700 Club and Christian Coalition fame, used his mailing list of devoted Christian followers and contributors to solicit recruits for an MLM company he founded in 1991. In a video promotion, Robertson claimed that multi-level marketing is "one of the greatest expressions of the Biblical principles of prosperity that I know of..." Going on to quote Scripture, Robertson signed up nearly 20,000 distributors to sell discount coupon books and advertised the company at political rallies for his Christian Coalition members.

"Christian Coalition Members – You've Made Your Political Voice Heard!!!" stated the ad. "Now Make Your Economic Voice Heard!!!" Robertson urged his followers on with the cry, "With God there is no cap. In the multi-level business, the sky is the limit." Calling the building of his financial empire God's Marvelous System of Money Management, Robertson backed himself up by asserting in one of his books that, if you give some of your money to the Lord, He will eventually shower you with earthly blessings.

When the wholly Robertson-owned MLM operation subsequently fell into financial misfortune, many distributors were left with discontinued products and lost investments, some totaling more than $10,000. Yet, in order to maintain business, Robertson simply switched the marketing program to vitamins and other food supplements including one nutritional drink called American Whey. Robertson's newly structured MLM company is now called KaloVita, The Good Life Company, which continues to diversify its offerings to include such products as Sea of Galilee face creams and mud masks. The Florida Attorney General's Office began an investigation of KaloVita in the fall of 1992 but, according to *Newsweek* magazine, KaloVita continues to diversify its product offerings.[34]

With these kinds of examples readily available across America, it becomes obvious how much of a kissing cousin MLM is to pyramid schemes and how closely we must look to determine the differences. The June 1987 edition of *Money* magazine offered an investigative overview of the growing MLM movement. The magazine concluded that while some multi-level firms are legitimate, scores of them are not. *Money* finished, "Every day, unscrupulous founders of multi-level companies prey on some of

---

[34] Michael Isikoff and Mark Hosenball, "With God There's No Cap." *Newsweek*, October 3, 1994, pp. 42-44.

the most gullible and often most financially troubled people in our society."

The three month long study by *Money* asserted, "The multi-level marketing mess must be contained if not halted" and it offered five suggestions for cleaning up both the multi-level business and its image: (1) Better industry self-policing through a national trade association; (2) Passage of a federal multi-level marketing law that sets standards and delineates the differences between a legal company and an illegal pyramid scheme and prevents owners of illegal companies from starting other multi-level firms; (3) Better enforcement from the FTC on deceptive sales practices in MLMs; (4) Zealous enforcement by the FDA to halt fraudulent claims made by MLM nutrition companies, and (5) New state laws requiring MLMs to file disclosure statements to enable prospective customers or distributors to find out about the business experience of the founder and the company's capitalization.[35]

An article which appeared in Florida on page one of the September 12, 1991 *Hallandale Digest* might shed further light on this dilemma. The article, entitled "Multi-Level Marketing, American Dream or Scam,"[36] listed the four guidelines that the Florida Attorney General's office uses to distinguish a legal multi-level company from an illegal pyramid scam as follows: (1) You are asked to pay a registration fee or purchase a training or sales kit for more than $200; (2) The firm retains the right to sell other distributorships in your area; (3) You can advance in the firm by selling new distributorships; (4) More than half the firm's income is derived from the activity of recruiting new associates or more than half of their time is spent recruiting new associates.

---

[35] "The Mess Called Multi-Level Marketing." *Money*, June, 1987, pp. 136-160.

[36] "Multi-Level Marketing, American Dream or Scam" *Hallandale Digest*, Florida, September 12, 1991.

The article noted that the fourth criterion is the most important to evaluate. In other terms, whether it's MLM or a pyramid scheme, it is imperative to simply and honestly make the assessment.

Economics 2000?

Thus far, we have addressed the values, ethics and beliefs that undergird pyramid schemes and multi-level marketing and their historical connectedness to New Age thinking. We have examined MLM's questionable legality and its close association with pyramid schemes. And we have looked at its commercializing influence on personal and family life and its compromising effect on the integrity of some professions. To respond to MLM's ever-present and forceful solicitations, one must finally speak directly to the issues of its economics.

The economic evaluation of MLM must lead to the determination of whether or not the business is a sound and practical one in which to invest. The MLM company itself may be toeing the legal line and it may be enjoying robust profitability. But, these corporate indicators do not address the question of whether or not it truly offers a reasonable return on investment to its distributors who are legally and financially independent operators.

Examples abound of businesses which are legal and profitable but which most people agree fail the test of economic legitimacy. Consider for example, auto dealerships that pressure and take advantage of naive buyers; the selling of worthless advertising media to unseasoned new business owners and risky securities to elderly and uninformed investors; useless and expensive job search services sold to the unemployed; and countless others where salesmanship sustains the enterprises in lieu of substance.

All solicitations for financial investment and employment opportunities are normally subjected to systematic scrutiny. Yet, when a solicitation such as MLM's is wrapped in spiritual principles of divine prosperity and stirring appeals to the ideals of free enterprise or when the solicitation is delivered by charismatic speakers at euphoric rallies with thousands of people wildly applauding and endorsing the program or when the sales pitch is personally presented by a close friend or relative, the requirement for sober economic evaluation is even more necessary. Therefore, to put the MLM industry into its proper business and economic context, some background on the dynamics of wholesale distribution may be helpful.

America represents a mature economy and penetrating markets in such a system is much more costly than in a young, hungry economy. The glut of goods flowing into the U.S. from all over the world makes name brand identity less and less important. Quality can be closely matched. Style can be easily imitated. The options for advertising are exploding through hundreds of new cable television stations, specialized magazines, international sporting event sponsorships, direct mail, local radio, celebrity endorsements and the global Internet.

Also facing every marketer is the fact that new prospects are harder and harder to locate, sell and maintain. Consumers are inundated with buying options and overloaded with information. Customers are mobile and brand loyalty is down. There are multiple challenges to answer. How can your vitamin pill, weight loss formula, laundry soap, long distance telephone service, water filter, algae food supplement, subliminal tape, travel bureau services, mouth wash, facial make-up or herbal laxative ever find its place on the shelf of this vast and already overcrowded global bazaar?

Keeping all this in mind, distribution emerges as one of the most powerful determinants of economic success. In mature markets, this aspect of business normally overshadows factors of technology, brand name identification, even product quality and price.

Economically speaking, MLM presents itself as a distribution channel ideally suited for today's mature marketplace. Its promoters say it is the most modern and progressive way of distributing products. It's called the wave of the future and is said to be replacing the traditional distribution channels such as wholesale-to-retail or manufacturer-to-dealer.

To some manufacturers or service providers, MLM's economic power or attraction is that it can deliver products to thousands of people even in these mature market conditions with virtually no sales and marketing cost to the supplier. The multiple levels of distributors bear all their own sales and marketing costs.

The focus of this study, however, is not on whether you should sell your product through an MLM channel or not but rather on whether or not you should become part of that channel as a distributor. For many manufacturers, the fate of individuals in the distribution channel is of no economic consequence. In MLM, this harsh economic fact is carried beyond all limits known in conventional business. As will be shown, the success of the few in MLM absolutely depends upon the failures of the many. The laws of mathematics require this. If more than a tiny percentage were to succeed, the factors of exponential growth would quickly exhaust the market. And, so, MLM distributors by the thousands must be and are replaced as quickly as they fail and drop out.

Pulling and Pushing Products

In distribution strategy, channels push products when the customer is loyal to the distributor but does not have a strong brand name preference. Under these market circumstances, the distributor has an increasing opportunity to sell its favorite brand to its customers. When brand names are preferred by customers, the manufacturer will engage in marketing efforts to pull the product through the distributor. Less is required or expected of the distributor towards selling the product.

Applying this basic principle of distribution to MLM, we see a channel that sells products with little established brand loyalty or uniqueness that would generate substantial customer demand. A survey of the MLM industry's array of bestsellers will reveal very few values that could not be found from many other sources. If a product was truly unique, exceptionally better priced or of measurably superior quality, it would find its way to market in the traditional manner. In fact, it would be sought after by these much larger channels.

A cursory review of MLM's most typical offerings reveals some common characteristics. Most are repeatedly purchased consumable goods or services that require no technical support or service from the distributors. They are usually unregulated by the government. In units, they are low cost goods but, over time, they grow to require substantial sums of money. Frequently, they are products such as food supplements which promise to ward off illnesses and whose performance claims cannot be easily tested

As a further verification of the MLM push model of distribution, we see the increasingly common phenomenon of entire MLM downlines switching companies, transferring from one brand or type of product to another. Indeed, many new MLMs are started in this manner illustrating that MLM takes the market condition where brand name identification has little pulling power to a remarkable extreme. In MLM, the product's brand is not only unimportant, the product itself is fundamentally irrelevant except to legalize the enterprise.

Pushing Irrelevant Products

The extreme pushing model of MLM reveals itself in MLM's famous recruitment techniques. Here this industry has far surpassed in relentlessness and manipulation all other contenders selling used car sales, time-share vacation apartments or life insurance. Those who have experienced the high energy of an MLM sales pitch – and who hasn't? – will understand its extraordinary pushing power. Leveraging friendships and relatives, staging huge recruitment rallies with political and show business celebrities as speakers and engaging in wildly exaggerated product performance claims, MLM ferociously pushes its products into market. Seldom asked is the question that any would-be distributor should ask, "Who is the market?"

Anyone who has attended an MLM recruitment meeting will testify that, whatever the product happens to be, it is presented as largely incidental. In actual experience at Amway meetings, for example, products were barely mentioned while the economic potential of building a pyramid sales organization was zealously promoted.

When the product is stressed in MLM recruitment meetings, it is often grossly exaggerated as one which sells itself. Frequently it is said to have nearly miraculous powers. The product is presented in hyperbolic terms to make the case that it will be easy to build the sales organization which, as opposed to retailing the product, is the true source of income for the distributors. Even the most naive and inexperienced recruit understands that door-to-door selling of these goods would be an unattractive or unexciting prospect.

Therefore, economically speaking, MLM is not a consumer-driven business as is the case with other distribution channels such as wholesale warehouses, superstores and shopping malls or mail order catalogues and telemarketing operations. Each of these competitive channels of distribution offers the customer a special advantage in price, convenience, product availability or service. These various distribution channels develop and are shaped out of specific customer needs.

MLM's method of distribution, on the other hand, did not develop in response to consumer needs. With five or six levels of passive profit-takers, MLM is not an efficient or economical means of bringing products to market. If the entire MLM industry today vanished from the earth, the buying public could easily, immediately and without additional cost acquire the same or comparable products elsewhere. Consumer-driven requirements for price, quality and service – the factors that are reshaping all other distribution channels – are mostly immaterial in MLM because its products are immaterial to the channel's growth.

The reasonable business person must ask, if MLM is not driven by customer needs or demands and, if its products and services do not drive the sales, what purpose does it serve in the economy? The answer is all too clear.

When the MLM solicitation is finally reduced to its barest essentials, it is seen that it exists solely to serve the economic needs and hopes of its own sales force, an approach which is diametrically opposed to all other forms of distribution which are customer-driven.

Investigative reporters and state regulators have universally concluded that the MLM industry sprang up in America and elsewhere in the world out of the need for many to earn additional money rather than as a result of the financial needs or wants of the buying public. Economic insecurity, unemployment, under-employment, corporate restructuring, national recessions – these are the motivating factors leading millions to become MLM distributors, thereby, sustaining the industry.

It is easy to see how the person frightened for his or her job, the unemployed person, the person in debt or the bitter, frustrated employee is a vulnerable prospect for MLM's bombastic and reassuring propositions for high income and financial independence. In truth, because of this unique MLM sales environment, *Money* magazine stated in its investigative report on the MLM industry, "Every day, unscrupulous founders of multi-level companies prey on some of the most gullible – and often most financially troubled – people in our society."

A Channel Without Customers

Who then is buying MLM products? Distributors. And, who do the distributors sell these products to? Other distributors. Then does any of it ever get out of the system to the buying public? Only an insignificant amount, all by design. There is little focus on retail sales because there is scant purpose in it or economic justification for it. Rather than basing its sales on the advantages it offers to its customers, e.g., price, convenience or quality, the primary emphasis is placed on the investment opportunity to become an MLM distributor.

This is a critical distinction that those who consider entering such a channel must be encouraged to understand. They have not been enrolled to push the product through to the buying public or even to deliver goods that a manufacturer is pulling with marketing and sales promotions. Instead, in MLM, the distributors themselves are the market on whom the goods are pushed.

As an economic institution, MLM poses as a channel which delivers goods to the market when in reality it is an institution that creates a market out of people who need jobs or extra income. Its well-honed marketing tools include the delivery of offers of extraordinary income coupled with the skillful use of fear and insecurity, a powerful set of tools, indeed.

We can see that products do not flow through this channel but rather to it. MLM must, therefore, be measured not by its efficiency in delivering products to market since that is not why it exists but by the value it delivers to its own family of distributors, its very customers. Their positions as distributors are the true products delivered by the system. It is their needs that the institution promises to fulfill and they are, at the core, its very purpose for existing.

Ignoring Supply and Demand

In the conventional distribution business, the most flagrant short-term and profit-driven abuse that damages the manufacturer/distributor relationship is the over-saturation of a market area with too many distributors. This results from unregulated and uncontrolled authorization of distributors which in the franchise world, for example, is legally prohibited by federal disclosure laws and contracts.

It is a well-proven fact that a manufacturer or national distributor can engage in this abuse and, for a time, reap great benefits at the expense of unwitting sub-distributors whose personal investments are exploited. For a time, even for years, this abuse of relationship can appear quite productive and profitable for the manufacturer or master distributor. Each sale to a distributor is considered a final sale whether it ever reaches an end-user or not. And, more distributors mean more warehouses, more sales outlets and more product in the channel.

Only over time is this abuse revealed for what it is – a short term strategy, a manipulation and, some would say, a fraud without lasting business validity. However, it is quite well-understood that a corrupted or faulty system can, in fact, make some people very rich, albeit, at the expense of others. This is legal and all but impossible to prevent. Only by employing experience and wisdom that are accompanied by a little bit of luck can a distributor avoid falling into this business pitfall. It is often the lure of a hot new product that leads distributors into this unprofitable situation. The result is that they end up with overloaded inventories while swimming in a sea of competitors all with the same dealership selling to the same customers.

In the conventional business community, economics as well as ethics require that extraordinary effort be put into predicting market sizes in order to avoid excessive inventory, over-capacity of manufacturing or, on the other hand, inability to meet demand. Any of these scenarios can spell economic disaster for the manufacturer and distributor.

Indeed, distributors in almost all industries are organized into trade associations and are represented by those who lobby for them against over-saturation of distributorships in the interests of functioning within the laws of supply and demand. They monitor their industries and report instances of distribution abuses or manipulation which is to say they look out for anyone who would violate these economic laws as long years of experience have shown where violation, ultimately, leads.

Regarding the MLM scheme in which we have been solicited to invest our funds as well as those of our friends and families, the ordinary requirements for anticipating market size, regulating the distribution channels and avoiding over-capacity are completely ignored. As one analyst described it, "MLM is inherently unstable. It is set up by design to go blindly past the saturation point."[37]

While this is theoretically true, it must also be said that the MLM company itself does not have to collapse. Rather, the consequences are typically borne by the revolving distributor pool. Distributors, for a time, can be replaced with new recruits who have no knowledge of local market conditions or the nature of the system they have entered. Meanwhile, their collective investments permit the MLM company to endure and even appear to be vigorous and healthy.

---

[37] For a thorough rebuttal of MLM's value proposition for distributors, see "What's Wrong with MLM" at World Wide Web site http://www.best.com/~vandruff/mlm.html. This home page provides an excellent reference for other MLM-related materials including its cult aspects, the current class action lawsuit against Amway distributors, the questionable business of selling motivational tapes and other success materials to MLM recruits, official government warnings and directions to other sources on the Internet published by the MLM industry.

Because MLM has, by design, no mechanism for controlling distribution and, therefore, will not prevent over-saturation of an area, the system must compensate in some way to survive the chaotic future it is creating. One way is to continuously misrepresent the opportunity offered to the distributors. [38] Thus, the standard MLM presentation claims to offer extraordinary opportunity beyond that of all other jobs or careers. The promoter never allows that an area might already be saturated or that it soon will be. The solicitation focuses exclusively on the extraordinary sales opportunity.

How could a market never be over-saturated if distributors can be endlessly added to the network? Only if the potential for over-saturation is not real but theoretical. Then it must be concluded that the program is not at all the extraordinary sales opportunity it is sold as but a remarkably difficult and unwise one. This fatal reality which could destroy any chance for MLM's growth is carefully concealed through systematic misrepresentation.

History has unquestionably demonstrated that the vast majority of people who attempt to succeed at MLM will fail. Yet, rather than being characterized by its massive failure rate, MLM promotion has succeeded in presenting itself to the world as the source of unlimited opportunity.

A profile article on the Amway Corporation in *Forbes* magazine reported that the average Amway distributor earns a gross profit of around $780 a year. Expenses for such things as phone, travel, postage and publicity materials must be paid for from this income. The article went on to add that the average distributor also personally consumes

---

[38] In fact, Amway's recruitment efforts became so widespread they had to develop an even more oblique enrollment technique of not revealing the company's name to those being solicited. Guests were asked to come to a meeting only to hear about an incredible opportunity.

$1,068 worth of Amway goods and that only 19% of Amway goods are sold to people not affiliated with the company. The article further stated that about half of Amway's 1.8 million distributors drop out of active sales after a year.[39]

In a 1983 presentation, the CBS television program, *60 Minutes*, presented the findings of a study by the Wisconsin Attorney General's office of 20,000 Amway distributors in that state. The study revealed that less than 1% of Amway's Wisconsin distributors earned a total of $14,000 a year gross income and, of these, the average actually reported a net loss after expenses. The *60 Minutes* report on Amway concluded that the company "sells hope not soap."

MLM asks its investors to give abundantly of their time. Time, of course, is the one commodity which can never be recouped. While it is true that an MLM distributorship requires little start-up capital in cash, it does require a massive infusion of capital in time. Weekends, evenings, social gatherings, church attendance, family reunions all now represent additional work time for the new MLM distributor. If the required time is not available to a new investor due to other work or family responsibilities, the chances for success are absurdly remote. In other words, the venture will be fatally under-capitalized.

While time spent on unsuccessful ventures can eventually be written off to life and new labors begun, MLM asks for one more investment which cannot be written off. It asks its investors to capitalize on their personal relationships. Taking the plunge into a high risk venture can be treated as poor judgment but also a valuable experience. Nothing ventured, nothing gained. It is a far different thing, however, to pull close friends and family members into the venture with you. The capital of trusted

---

[39] Paul Klebnikov, "The Power of Positive Inspiration." *Forbes*, December 9, 1991, pp. 244-249.

friendships and the harmony of family can never be fully regained once commercially exploited.

The question for an investor to raise is whether MLM is worthy of the time, money and requirements of commercializing personal relationships. Though millions of people cannot explain exactly what actually happened in their failed attempts in MLM, they often can say with conviction the enterprise was simply not worth it.

In the mainstream world of product distribution as represented by the National Association of Wholesale-Distributors, a system of unregulated and unlimited distributorship authorization is economic suicide for a manufacturer and an economic trap for a distributor. Laws of supply and demand, the dynamics of good faith dealer/manufacturer relationships and the requirement to achieve organizational stability for both dealer and manufacturer necessitate regulating and nourishing, not endlessly adding to and churning the network of distributors.

Does MLM have some special power to transcend these forces and laws of economics? Yes, if you believe in alchemy.

Economic Alchemy

*Of the people who have
most distinguished themselves
in this unprofitable pursuit are
men of all ranks, characters and
conditions: the truth-seeking
but erring philosopher; the
ambitious prince and the needy
noble, who have believed in it,
as well as the designing
charlatan, who has not believed
in it, but has merely made the
pretension to it the means of
cheating his fellows and living
upon their credulity.*[40]

— *Charles Mackay on
the history of alchemy*

The medieval science that dedicated its
proponents to transmuting base metals into gold was
known as alchemy. Attracting some of Europe's best
minds from theologian Thomas Aquinas to scientist
Roger Bacon, the history of this alleged technology
includes the long search for a mystical substance
called the philosopher's stone. This imaginary
material was thought to transform common metals
such as lead into silver or gold. Turning into far
more than just primitive chemistry, a sophisticated
philosophy grew up around the belief in alchemy
including a belief that it held the keys to perfect
health and the means to indefinitely prolong life.

---

[40] Charles Mackay, *Extraordinary Popular Delusions and the Madness
of Crowds.* London: Richard Bentley, New Burlington Street, 1841. This
remarkable book has enjoyed re-publication several times including the
1932 edition with a foreword by financier Bernard Baruch. Among the
popular delusions historically chronicled and analyzed are pyramid
schemes, alchemy, witchcraft and the First Crusade.

The discovery of its secrets in both the laboratory and in philosophical inquiry was the obsession of intellectuals, kings and popes.

While never delivering the much-pursued philosopher's stone, alchemists' efforts did result in discoveries of new elements and compounds. In addition, their philosophical inquiries were revered for the fact that they penetrated beyond what could only be seen with the eye to a higher level of enlightened understanding – a metaphysics that governed material life. Thus, the writings and perspectives of these alchemists contained profound and lasting wisdom.

Alchemy's worldly promises of cheating death, curing all disease and procuring unlimited wealth, however, also attracted some of history's most famous liars and frauds. Many of Europe's greatest courts and clerics were swept up in this folly and today, as a result, the recorded fraud and ignorance of that era today far overshadow any of its contributions to science and philosophy.

Transmuting Labor into Wealth

Correspondingly, MLM employs a form of alchemy in its economic promises and, like the philosopher's stone, pyramid math offers only an imaginary or theoretical concept. The promise of a pyramid sales organization being able to effortlessly and continuously transmute labor into wealth cannot be experienced in reality. As we will see, such a structure will quickly collapse as a result of exponential growth. When it does appear to be functioning, it is only on the basis of false promises and futile efforts of those on the chain below. In truth, it is a seductive riddle not an economic structure. Yet, public belief in it can generate billions in profit for its Merlin-like promoters.

Alchemy's promises of limitless wealth, perfect health and prolonged life are uncannily similar to MLM success prophecies. In the thousands of alchemists' experiments of repeatedly but futilely mixing and heating their concoctions, there is a sad resemblance to millions of MLMers manipulating their friends, harassing neighbors, studying their self-improvement manuals, listening to subliminal success tapes and attending euphoric pep rallies.

The wealth and power that accrued to the alchemists, of course, did not come from converting metal to gold or from prolonging life or curing disease. It was gained by attracting the support of those who believed it could accomplish these miracles.

MLM is a system that, likewise, is an illusion of what it purports to be. It lives only on the strength of the belief of its latest enrollees. The much-promised success is founded upon the hopes and failures of those on the bottom of the chain. If many succeed, its structure will immediately collapse under the weight of the countless members who would quickly consume whole markets. To endure, it must generate millions of failures. By its power to attract these failures whose money enriches a handful of promoters, it creates the illusion of validity and enhances its power to attract more. By definition, it can never stabilize or sustain its distributors. Only by churning millions in and out of the system can it continue. Its growth is sustained only with continuous and pervasive misrepresentation of market realities or through other emotional or intellectual distractions. The so-called success of some of its distributors is founded upon this illusion and misrepresentation.

Enchanted by the Message of Hope and Salvation

Kings and princes commonly retained alchemists and financed their studies and laboratories. How could such an illusion have captured the imagination of Europe's intellectuals and sustained itself for so long?

Alchemy's credibility in the face of centuries of failed experiments can be largely attributed to its close association with a rich spiritual philosophy. Alchemists took the profound and made it profane with their false promises and vainglorious goals. Alchemy enchanted medieval Europe not on the strength of its primitive science but rather with its esoteric philosophy which linked the mystical with the material world. It offered an explanation of the nature of all matter. And its philosophical concepts were powerfully rooted in the medieval world where mysticism pervaded all aspects of life.

Alchemy offered hope and promise and the light of understanding in a world in which death came early and disease and poverty were the certain plight of all but a privileged few. The great alchemists of history were revered and honored for their optimistic and powerful promises to unlock the secrets of the Universe for the betterment of humanity.

Likewise, MLM, a system founded on the necessary failure of millions, endures and grows because of its philosophical messages. MLM has capitalized upon America's modern day version of mysticism, a legacy of Emerson and Thoreau's Transcendentalism. It offers a message of personal freedom and exalted individualism which challenges each person to be the master of his or her own destiny, free to choose and to create, no longer the victim of circumstance. Modern American mysticism links the mind to matter where enlightened thinking can reshape reality. Vision can be magically manifested. Financial success in MLM, like the transmuting of lead to gold in alchemy, is the goal of this mystical power, the highest of all achievements and proof of personal alignment with God. It is offered as spiritual deliverance.

Just as alchemy's failures were always attributed to the incompetence or inadequacy of the experimenter and never to alchemy's flawed and fantastic claims, failure to succeed financially in the MLM system is treated as a sign of mystical discordance and is the responsibility only of the defeated distributors rather than of a delusive MLM program.

Thus cast under the spell of its belief system and mesmerized by its promises, MLM enrollees can scarcely evaluate the bogus economics of the system they have entered. They have become just like the medieval princes who, listening to the alchemist's esoteric dissertation on the nature of matter, could not grasp the implausibility of transmuting lead to gold.

Wisely, in later years, alchemists concluded that the philosopher's stone did not exist in reality but was only the symbol for spiritual enlightenment. Health, wealth and even prolonged life, they decided, were available to all simply through study and contemplation. The alchemists' basic philosophy contained timeless wisdom. Its fraudulence lay only in the manner in which it was erroneously or deceptively applied.

MLM, the alchemy of the business world, is not a legitimate, sustainable economic institution any more than alchemy was a science. Like alchemy, MLM is an industry which thrives only on the seductive appeal of its promises and its adept association with a compelling philosophy. It is a chimera whose temptations are, indeed, difficult to penetrate or resist. Blessed with business legality, wrapping itself in a New Age philosophy which celebrates human freedom and flaunting its false profits as ephemeral evidence of soundness and substance, it is understandable that millions of people fall under its spell. For those who become enchanted, it may take years to break MLMs incantations and get on with their lives in authentic expression of their personal dreams and values. As 19th century writer Charles MacKay wrote in the preface to his classic historical collection, *Extraordinary Popular Delusions*, "It will be seen that people go mad in herds while they only recover their senses slowly and one by one."

False Profits

Yet a Prophet Arrives
and a Bible Is Written

If the late Jerry Rubin,[41] former Chicago 7 revolutionary of the 60's and founder of the Yippie movement, was MLM's most notable prophet, *Wave 3: The New Era in Network Marketing* by Richard Poe can certainly be considered its current bible. Ranked #13 on *Business Week's* best-seller list of business-related publications in June, 1996, *Wave 3* is promoted at MLM rallies, quoted in MLM newsletters and cited as the final word on the economic value, historical development and future growth of this business system.

While *Wave 3* can be counted among the multitude of how-to-become-a-millionaire-in-MLM offerings on bookstore shelves today, its mission goes beyond this popular message becoming in its economic dissertation the *Das Kapital* of the network marketing industry. Placing MLM clearly at the pinnacle of capitalistic evolution, *Wave 3* codifies and confirms Jerry Rubin's 1990's prophecy of MLM's eventual dominance of American capitalism, the same system which Rubin in the 1960's had flamboyantly predicted would collapse. "There is a worldwide yearning for freedom," Rubin said. "Network marketing is about freedom – financial freedom, time freedom and personal freedom – to do and be whatever you want to do and be." Accordingly, if we choose to believe Rubin and *Wave 3* foretellings, in answer to these yearnings, MLM will soon dominate our national economy and providentially carry us all into its infrastructure and way of thinking.

---

[41] Jerry Rubin was, for a time, MLM's "most prominent cheerleader." He died in an automobile accident in 1994. See "New Age Capitalism" by Wesley J. Smith, *Home Office Computing*, August, 1992, p. 56-61.

"The impact network marketing... is having and will have on all our lives is genuinely transformational," claims Poe in *Wave 3*. "From a proactive and pioneering use of technology to a more humane, some say even spiritual, honoring of individual effort and personal freedom, network marketing will permeate our society and culture worldwide as few concepts born of business ever have." In other words, selling products to one another, the defining transaction of MLM as a distribution model, has been lifted to a new level of human endeavor.

The world according to *Wave 3* finds MLM companies replacing extended families and ancient ethnic identities. "Network marketing downlines," writes Poe, "often exhibit the same proclivities for worldwide organization, rapid global response and close personal ties as do the more familiar tribes like the Chinese or the Hasidim. MLM companies may someday resemble transnational states, whose treasuries rival those of powerful nations and whose 'citizens' work in unison on every continent of the earth, united only by a computer network and a common tribal vision."

To those who have studied MLM, this kind of prophetic rhetoric comes uncomfortably close to the cult-like domination that Amway has had over many of its core distributors, a perception which is well-founded. *Wave 3* supports its vision of an MLM-dominated world economy by authoritatively referring to the proclamation Amway founder Richard De Vos made to *Forbes* magazine. "Amway is more than a company... It's a movement," Poe quotes De Vos as saying. Poe goes on to remind us that Amway has long understood the power of tribal vision. "Its mass rallies open with the stirring strains of *Chariots of Fire*... they feature sermons on family life and the stars and stripes... No Amway distributor can ever forget that his company... stands for the American Way." Calling the MLM system a revolutionary movement complete with its own gods and heroes, Poe claims its mission will be expressed not in dollars and cents but in terms of the loftiest ideals.

In addition to providing six figure incomes to the various distributors whose lives are described in *Wave 3*, MLM is also credited with the return of the family. A wealthy Nu Skin distributor explains, "The big difference between us and other people that are trapped in traditional business is that we have a vehicle that allows us to be a family together. We really owe everything about our lives to this business."

Quoting one of MLM's prominent newsletter publishers, Poe puts forth the idea that network marketing may be the religion of the next millennium. "The ideal network marketing company should be a brotherhood of honest and hardworking folk whose lives center not around a corporate rat race but around friendship, service and communion with one another – not unlike the ideal church... But when the collection basket is passed, instead of you dropping money in, money drops out into your lap."

Can any of us avoid the predicted MLM future or choose not to participate in it? According to *Wave 3*, your resistance would not only be foolish but in vain. The author presents a future scenario in which every man, woman and child gets a computerized commission check every month for the hundreds of goods and services they are touting to family, friends and neighbors. Moreover, they get to purchase all those same goods and services themselves at a wholesale discount which can run as high as 50 percent.

At this point, Poe warns the non-participant, "You're beginning to suspect that you're the last person in America who pays full retail price for anything. Still, you resist. You say, 'We'll never give in. We'll never be network marketers. Never.' But, deep down inside, you know it's only a matter of time..."

Wave 3 goes on to describe MLM as a new and unconventional business system offering greater opportunity for wealth and leisure than any traditional employment or business ownership opportunity. Requiring no special knowledge, education or training, on closer examination, the basis for MLM is found largely in the writings of New Thought and self-help philosophers. The message springs from these origins to the MLMer that the only essential to success is faithful adherence to the established system of operation taught by the MLM leaders. *Wave 3* also shows it to be a social phenomenon which has become aligned with the ideals of personal freedom, entrepreneurship and individual liberty.

Leaning heavily on New Thought practices which include persuasion, training and the motivation of new recruits, the most potent factor for success in the MLM business is said to be personal attitude or belief. That being the case, a rigorous re-education of new recruits is integral to all MLM programs. The philosophical and educational tenets include systematic efforts to re-program the subconscious in order to shape and direct the future; the development of a mental habit of positive affirmations to bolster confidence; employment of creative visualization techniques to focus effort and energy on specific goals, most often the attainment of financial income or material possessions; and the upholding of a continuously optimistic attitude toward attracting supportive resources and people.

Behind all of this seemingly healthy self-development activity is the belief in a destiny of financial prosperity which is held to be God's ultimate intention for each individual. Here we finally encounter our old mentor, prosperity consciousness, taken together with mental conditioning and philosophic arguments to form the liturgy and doctrine of the MLM movement. Reaching a high personal income is treated as a kind of salvation in this religious-like business system. Mastering the philosophy is the necessary pathway to deliverance. New recruits are powerfully indoctrinated with these concepts through audio and video tapes, books, pamphlets, lectures, seminars and rallies in a manner resembling religious indoctrination.

In fact, many MLM companies go on to make a major business out of the sale of personal development training materials. For example, Amway's largest distributor, Dexter Yager of Charlotte, North Carolina, owns his own publishing company which reportedly sells more than $35 million of these materials each year to all new Amway recruits in his downline. Amway distributors are commonly encouraged to participate in a tape-a-week program sold by Yager's publishing company, Internet, Inc. Pressure and requirements on new recruits by Yager's Amway distribution group to purchase the training tapes eventually prompted a class action law suit against Amway and its two largest distributors, Dexter Yager and Bill Britt accusing them of operating a pyramid scheme.

On another interesting note, Nightingale-Conant Publishing Company, the largest publisher of self-help, positive thinking audio tapes and books, has itself become a major product line for one of the fastest growing MLMs, Nutrition for Life, led by marketer Kevin Trudeau. However, in April of 1996, the Attorney General of Illinois accused Trudeau of operating an illegal pyramid scheme and gained a court injunction against Nutrition for Life. This effectively halted the promotion of a part of the Nutrition for Life marketing program which required new investors to purchase $100 of educational tapes per month.[42]

In similar fashion, one of the newest MLMs in the country, The People's Network, has made dissemination of educational and philosophical materials its main product line. Information is distributed via satellite television upon the investor's

---

[42] This payment was automatically deducted from the new distributor's checking account or charged to his credit card.

purchase of a small satellite dish and payment of a monthly subscription fee.

As has been herein suggested, *Wave 3* notes that until the 1980's, MLM was overwhelmingly characterized by one company, Amway, which represents the first wave. This phase lasted until 1979 when the Federal government dropped the case it had waged against Amway upon failing to prove that it was an illegal pyramid scheme. The result in the 1980's was a proliferation of many new MLM companies, nearly all built on the Amway model. This represented the second wave and, correspondingly, the same period in which the national craze for pyramid schemes reached the New Age community. The term Wave 3 refers to the current stage of development in which most MLM companies distribute via computer thus freeing distributors from having to personally stock and deliver inventory. Additionally, corporate computers now track downlines and manage many other financial and legal responsibilities for their distributors.

None of the hype, justifications or descriptions of the MLM system in *Wave 3* is new. It has been presented at Amway meetings for decades as parts of the promise of a unique money making system. In true MLM hallmark fashion, extraordinary income for ordinary people is tantalizingly presented in *Wave 3*. Typical of all MLM promotion, the glamorous lifestyles of prosperous and happy distributors are featured throughout the book. The tools and methods for success are, once again, described as simple and easy to master. The odds of success are offered as high and efforts at reaching same are characterized as worthy of time and financial investment.

Predictably, the ultimate success of the system is depicted as historical destiny. Failure to join is viewed as a foolish, fear-driven decision based on negativity or poor judgment and promising later regret. Pursuing alternatives to MLM such as conventional career development, learning a trade, seeking employment in a major corporation, delving into other self-employment enterprises or simply focusing on spending less and saving more are depicted as unwise strategies that are pitifully short-sighted, lacking in imagination and doomed to failure.

Wave 3 is simply the latest of a number of prophetic and heraldic books employed in the massive MLM recruitment process. Many of the previous ones came from the Amway founders or their largest distributors. Like its predecessors, *Wave 3* is written to persuade on an absolute and grand scale. MLM is presented as a universal church, protector of the nuclear family or replacement for the extended family and the fullest expression of the American Way. All in all, MLM is positioned as the new phase of capitalism which will eventually engulf all commerce. MLM is offered as a system in which selling takes on spiritual dimensions, becoming a form of communion among a brotherhood, rivaling in its power the 4,000 years of history that support the Hasidim or the millennia of Chinese culture. *Wave 3* is, then, today's bible of the orthodox MLM movement.

To the uninitiated, *Wave 3* may appear to be a new voice, positioning MLM as not just an investment proposition that has been around for more than thirty years but as a new cultural force and an economic inevitability. Rather than focusing exclusively on the concepts of individual success, *Wave 3* places MLM in a wider sociological context discussing it alongside the Communist economic system, modern forms of tribalism, the "greening of America," today's new emphasis on family values and such popular social trends flextime and electronic networking. As a forward look, even its title infers a clever association with *The Third Wave*, Alvin Toffler's well-known treatise on future trends.

A Dissenter Speaks

How then does one review a bible which, by definition, is founded on faith? It could be muckraked and exposed but the faithful would only cling to core beliefs even as the historical validity and literal truthfulness of their scriptures were revealed to be mythical.

Perhaps the far better grasp of such a document can be reached in light of the experience and perspective of a former apostle of MLM, now a dissenter. Enter Stephen Butterfield, a former MLM true believer who dedicated two years of his life to building an Amway downline distribution system. Despite successful upward movement, Butterfield, like millions of other enrollees, eventually abandoned the effort. What distinguishes him from countless others is that Butterfield took the time to look back and reconcile his Amway experience with his core values.

Written over a decade ago, Butterfield's courageous and pioneering exposé of the Amway corporation, *Amway, the Cult of Free Enterprise*, remains in print today. Its publishers say that this autobiographical account of a college professor and musician drawn to Amway in the classic manner stands as a text offering unique perspective in a field that is raucous with hyperbole, enrollment and persuasive promotions.

"I wanted income security," wrote Butterfield, now deceased. "I liked the idea of making money, lots of it, without having to show up for work. If it (Amway) worked, I wanted to be on the bandwagon. I wanted to be plucking money from the money tree, not sitting on the outside of the circle chewing pits while others feasted. I couldn't buy a house, an airline ticket or a good suit. I always drove a settle-for car, no other kind existed for me, and I got used to the taste of soybeans."

Amway's promises of income security, luxury and leisure drew Butterfield in initially but he became driven by the larger vision portrayed by Amway leaders. This religious-like vision promoted the idea of helping mankind while encouraging the growth of a more egalitarian society in which greater numbers of people would have access to a higher quality of life and where a strong bond of community and a love-thy-neighbor sentiment could reflect itself in the business marketplace.

Butterfield had already worked for the advancement of these values in the labor union movement and was active in his local campus union for university employees. His understanding of Amway as a vehicle for the furtherance of this vision makes his chronicle an even more appropriate counterpoint to *Wave 3* as it challenges the basis of MLM's dedication to the advancement of these very same values.

The concept of a benevolent, religion-like movement focused on noble deeds such as helping the needy and providing spiritual fulfillment is what initially attracted Butterfield, a man who was already committed to social justice and a wider access to a decent livelihood for more of the people of America. What, then, did he find over two years of seeking this vision through MLM?

In fairness, it must be pointed out that Butterfield's ideals were not in complete alignment with MLM from the beginning. His first great challenge was in trying to adapt to the notion that accumulation of personal wealth was a part of the spiritual dimension. Then, as he attended early training seminars, he observed that most of the training was not about selling techniques or the explanation of product features and benefits. Rather it was about adopting the proper attitude, for attitude drives everything, he was told.

At each meeting he heard, "Your Dream is the reason you are in the business. Much of the Seminar, like the Plan, is devoted to building the Dream." However, this Dream, Butterfield discovered, was not a personal one. It had to conform to a narrowly stereotyped model, a kind of franchise dream. "It is a thoroughly consumerist and materialist craving which the leaders do everything to instill into their distributor force: driving Cadillacs and motor homes... arousing the envy of neighbors. Traveling first class to Hawaii and being waited on by servants.

"A Dream that could not be satisfied by money... would have no place here..." he mused. "Thoreau's concept that it might be more unselfish to employ yourself in your kitchen rather than accumulate wealth to employ someone else there, would seem incomprehensible within this flag-draped hall (the training rally place)." Nonetheless, Butterfield adopted the new vision of a better world in which "there is no conflict between being rich and being saved. If there was anything wrong with diamonds, God would not use them to decorate heaven. You must have money to perform good deeds."

Butterfield went on in the Amway training program to learn that the "ABCs of Success" are "Attitude, Belief and Commitment." Success in this lesson was always spelled out as $U¢¢E$$. Attitude was the key which must be guarded. "Don't let anyone steal your Attitude," Butterfield was constantly advised. He was continuously cautioned against the dangers of the Negative. Negative was defined as "whatever influence weakens your belief and commitment in the business." Soon he learned that the world of the Negative was a vast universe of potential bad influences or "stinking thinking."

Anyone who criticized the program, used competitive products, had personal doubts or questions, showed reluctance to attend seminars or refused to buy training and motivation tapes all fell within the realm of the Negative. The much touted liberty and pursuit of happiness, Butterfield learned, was a narrow road, indeed.

At this point, Butterfield's core values about helping people came to his aid, allowing him to consider the thought that his achieving personal financial success could be a step toward making the world a better place. He accepted the concept of selling products in the new context of helping people to improve their lives even though the products were more expensive than competitive brands. His first major hurdle in living this new way came when he started recruitment efforts among his personal friends and relatives. Butterfield did, indeed, encounter personal resistance when approaching friends which he overcame and then pursued the program as he was advised. He drew up his "warm" list and went after the people on it. He found the process a life-changing experience.

"Amway begins to change your life the first time you approach your friends and family members to sell the product or recruit them into the business," he wrote. "When you put a friend on a prospect list, then you are guiding that friendship into a preconceived direction. The friendship is no longer primary; it is a means to an end. You want something from that person. You want to sell her soap or to show her the plan," he so aptly described the shift in relationship.

"She meets you to go bowling, while you are rehearsing in your mind the script from a tape that will... get her talking about business and money. She is chatting about her kids, but you are waiting for the right moment to say, 'Isn't it tough nowadays to support kids on one income?' They think you are interested in their lives when you ask them about their schedule, but you are looking for a free evening to invite them over at eight o'clock to discuss an Exciting Idea."

Butterfield viewed the change as going from a relationship of equals to one of manipulator and manipulatee. "If you sponsor a friend, then the relationship is upline to downline – a completely prefabricated business association in which honest friendship gradually becomes impossible." Further, Butterfield believed that the danger of turning friends into customers and prospects was the biggest hurdle a distributor had to overcome and was, in fact, the cause of a sizable number of recruits dropping out of the program early. This obstacle to building the MLM system was powerfully and consistently addressed at seminars and training programs.

Amway offered new recruits the same rationale for enlistment that is presented in *Wave 3* – you're actually doing your friends a favor, guiding them toward a source of great income. Butterfield was told he should call his friends out of love for them. Amway, he was told, is love. Similarly, in *Wave 3*, MLM is called an expression of Christian charity.

"Your friends," Butterfield was told, "will either join or buy products or wish you success in your new endeavor. If they don't do any of these, then they are not your friends." As Butterfield discovered, many friends did not choose any of the three options. Some felt used. Some resented the leverage of their relationship for business. Some even criticized or rejected their friend's sales solicitations. Amway recruits were prepared for all these eventualities by the relentless portrayal of the Amway organization as a substitute for old friends and as an extended family to new recruits.

Accordingly, friends become unnecessary and expendable in the boundless search for downliners. "It is a favor to offer Amway to a friend, even an act of charity but, if the favor is refused, don't listen to that friend. The potential recruits know nothing and you don't need them anyway," Butterfield was counseled. He observed that acceptance of this view had a remarkable psychological effect on new recruits.

"We need human association and approval. If these needs are no longer met by our friends then they have to be met by the business. And, for those who stay in and achieve higher pins (indicators of sales growth), this is precisely what happens. We no longer need our former friends. We need the business instead. We need the approval of the upline Direct and the leader of the Seminars and Rallies. 'I lost my father and mother,' said a prominent

Emerald. 'My father still won't speak to me. But, in Amway, I acquired a whole new family.'"

The Amway distributor was also expected to serve as an exemplary model whose every word and action communicated sales support and encouragement. "I must be totally positive. No matter how I feel about the business," wrote Butterfield. "In response to questions I must always say, 'It's doing great! Fantastic!' Before Amway I might have been able to discuss feelings honestly with my friends. Now I say what is best calculated to sponsor them."

Beyond alienating friends and relatives in the process of transforming personal relationships into commercial associations, Butterfield learned firsthand the true nature of the much touted network. This is the social and financial structure that *Wave 3* calls a brotherhood, describing the interaction among its members as communion. Yet, in Amway as in all MLMs, this network was merely structured according to the compensation plan.

The Amway system of compensation is classified by *Wave 3* as the Stairstep/Breakaway type of plan. It is the dominant and most successful program in the MLM field and is emulated by other MLM giants such as Shaklee, Nu Skin and Quorum. In this system, as Butterfield learned, the network acts as a hierarchy not a brotherhood. According to *Wave 3*, "In a Stairstep/Breakaway plan, you succeed by ascending a staircase of achievement levels. At each step in your ascent, you are awarded a different honorific title such as Gold Executive or Three-Star Executive.

"Of all comp plans, the Stairstep/Breakaway provides the best opportunity for people to make it big. That's because (it) allows you to build a larger organization and to draw commission from a greater number of levels... Some Breakaway plans let you draw income from as deep as 20 levels down." Applying these organizational requirements to human interaction, Butterfield revealed that rigid control over distributors was required to not only prevent one level from raiding another but to actually eliminate even social contact between Breakaway "legs" of a downline.

Butterfield talked about how distributors were advised by Amway to build their downlines deep. That is, after sponsoring a new distributor and encouraging the new recruit to solicit others, the distributor was advised to focus on supporting and training the people under his new recruit. Why? Butterfield outlined the reasons for this strategy as follows:

1) "In case the new recruit drops out, the line can continue (minus his take of the commission).

2) "The way to motivate a personally sponsored leg is to build a fire under him. Business volume comes from the bottom up. If I keep adding new people under Jack in a straight line, his volume grows but he will not be able to keep that bonus money on that volume. By deepening the leg further, I make it necessary for him to add more width in order to profit from the work I have done for him.

3) "By working the downline of the person the distributor has sponsored, control is maintained. 'If I want to know if Jack is following my advice, I don't ask him directly. He might lie or get defensive. Instead, I befriend his downline and find out from them.'

4) "Jack may not be a leader. He might take years to become one and I would rather not wait that long. By working depth I can identify the potential leaders in his group... Then, if Jack is intractable and decides to run his own show, I can groom leaders downline from him and teach his people Dexter's way[43] whether he likes it or not. In fact, I can force Jack out entirely and still get a Direct from one of his legs."

Butterfield's education in the control and manipulation of his downline and the requirements

---

[43] Dexter Yager is the largest Amway distributor in the world under whom the greatest number of all Amway distributors operate.

on him to conform to the guidance and teaching of his upline took the mask off the most fundamental of all the myths espoused in *Wave 3*. The myth is that in MLM you own your own business. As he learned, the distributor is under great pressure to follow a rigid system of duplication. The system insists upon specific behavior, beliefs, convictions and use of approved rhetoric. The distributor must not only operate in conformity but must also think collectively at a level far beyond the limits imposed by corporate America upon its organization men.

The use of audio tapes warning against the world of the Negative, continuous training programs and seminars and a regular schedule of mass rallies were used for the purpose of imposing the conformity, regularity and control necessary to run a hierarchically-structured organization which is supposedly composed of independent entrepreneurs and autonomous business owners. *Wave 3* calls this hierarchical system in which as many as 20 levels of people seek to manipulate one another in a continuous recruitment process "the purest incarnation of the American spirit of free enterprise."

Wave 3 also offers many examples of exceptionally successful MLM distributors most with incomes of more than one-half million dollars per year. In the end, however, *Wave 3* does concede that, in reality, only the rarest few in the industry achieve this level of success. Yet, even with this admission of often paltry financial returns from MLM, *Wave 3* asserts that the system offers yet another unique reward to its adherents – freedom of time.

"Time will be one of the biggest issues and one of the most valued assets in the coming years," according to MLM spokesman, Jerry Rubin, in *Wave 3*. The book goes on to say that network marketing is one of the few known methods by which the masses can gain control over their daily schedules. It goes on to discredit the notion that major corporations will ever adopt family-friendly policies regarding work schedules.

Butterfield found a far different reality. "If you want to be a Diamond," said Dexter Yager on one of his training tapes, "fill your calendar. You ought to be out there drawing circles (showing the downline commission structure) six nights a week." Butterfield heard this tape after he had exhausted much of his warm list. He had called upon his friends and family and had little to show for it. Most had rejected the program outright. Some distanced themselves from him personally as he went about commercializing their relationships.

"I'm running out of friends" he told his sponsor.

"Your business won't take off until you start working with strangers," he was informed.

Soon he had purchased $30 worth of audio-training tapes on prospecting and cold-calling. Next, he was introduced to the lore of finding the "pearl" – that hoped-for experience of unexpectedly coming upon an extraordinary sales performer in the course of cold-calling. And, he went about developing lures to attract inquiries about MLM. He pretended to be waiting for someone and began mentioning, out loud, how surprised he was that this man was late for an interview for a great-paying job. This was intended to attract the attention of someone nearby who would, hopefully, inquire about the nature of the job offer.

Other lures included putting $100 bills in his wallet and announcing at check-out counters how good business was. This often drew inquiries about what type of good business he was in which gave him an opportunity to recruit. Another ploy was to continually mention how successful he was in avoiding taxes and, thereby, attract curiosity and conversation. Other tactics involved getting his wife to mention how well her husband was doing while stating that she did not know how to explain his business. This 'dumb wife' technique often led to her arranging appointments with potential recruits for her husband.

Butterfield followed the Amway prescription of guiding conversations to F-O-R-M: family, occupation, recreation and money. "My ear picked up any theme in a conversation that I could FORM. In talking about family, I listened for how I could use the natural family loyalties of a prospect to get him interested in the business. I wanted to know what he hoped to achieve for his family and whether his brother, sister, parents or children were ambitious types. I listened for any job dissatisfaction or longing for security. In talk about recreation, I prodded my target into describing his dreams and material desires. Money was the most straightforward subject and led right to the point. 'How would you like to double your income in twelve months?' Within a few weeks I was showing the Plan every night and had a drawer full of phone numbers I would never have time to follow up on."

Still having to maintain his daytime job, Butterfield found himself not only spending all his time working, he had also changed from being a freely interacting person to a highly-programmed operative who was essentially selling all the time. Free time no longer existed. In fact, Butterfield forsook any genuine interest in the people he signed up in order to maintain his new business relationship with them.

"In each case, friendship was limited only to what I could use to accomplish my goal. The justification given by Amway would be that in order to realize my Dream I must help the prospect realize his. But his Dream had to cost money, otherwise it would not be useful. And I had to play that Dream like a fish line, specifically to bring the prospect to my group. If he could realize his Dream by selling T-shirts or ski hats, I would make no profit on him and our Dream building association quickly evaporated. In the end, prospecting was more alienating than loneliness."

"What makes Amway different from most other sales work," Butterfield observed, "is the total, twenty-four-hour-a-day obsession with Building the Dream. The insurance person or the used car salesperson practices manipulation to sell policies or cars, not to save the world... Selling cars is not a path to salvation but only a way to make a living. The Amway distributor is a convert who wants to convert others. Human relationships outside of Amway have no meaning and are eventually dropped. In Amway, I must do more than sell a product; I must duplicate my Sponsor. And I must demand that my prospect duplicate me. Above, all, I must Believe."

Today, in what is now called the third wave of MLM, the number and scope of Amway-type companies has expanded greatly. All of them share the unique characteristic of selling a belief system for it is this system which sustains the effort and fuels the hope. Like Stephen Butterfield, the millions who are recruited eventually want to see the results, the promised luxury and leisure at the end of this mythical and transformational journey.

Butterfield got excited by the potential for wealth without labor, for leisure without worry. As his experience continued to contradict the promise of Amway, he still clung to the idea of eventually achieving a point where the labors would be transferred to those down the line.

Toward the end of his Amway odyssey, Stephen Butterfield realized what the true odds of success were. Using Amway's annual reports of sales in the U.S. and the number of people achieving Direct level, he concluded that only one to two percent of all those involved would ever achieve a compensation that could replace even a modest-paying job. Ninety-eight to ninety-nine percent would never make it. The percentage of those reaching the level of Diamond which offers an income of $50,000 to $100,000 is a mere .048%. "For one person to change (his social) class using the Amway vehicle, at least 2,083 new active people must be brought in, trained, motivated, programmed and supplied."

No wonder this system relied upon such intense and unrelenting recruiting, he realized. Failures by the thousands were needed to support the small group of winners at the apex of the hierarchy. In addition, Butterfield realized that there would be no point in time when the Amway channel of distribution could stabilize with its current participants. His calculation of the chances for financial success as a distributor in Amway were in fact more optimistic than other analyses subsequently put forth by government investigators.

The challenge here is to reconcile the glorious MLM prophecies and portrayals found in *Wave 3* with Stephen Butterfield's account of his unfortunate experience in the world's largest and most successful MLM company. Perhaps Butterfield resolved the matter when he later stated, "(The business) is sold as the American Dream but, for the average distributor, it's more like a nightmare."

The Butterfield experience, however similarly repeated among millions of recruits that have passed through the Amway program, does not directly refute the *Wave 3* interpretation. This is not a book of falsehoods and its testimonials from successful upliners are quite authentic. The MLM system has, as reported in *Wave 3*, expanded significantly since 1979 when Amway's legality was accepted by the Federal government. And, clearly, it has a power which has tapped, at least for a short time, the imaginations and energy of millions of Americans.

It is not in the finding of its literal misrepresentations that one can refute this book. In determining the truth, as with MLM itself, one must look not so much for any direct deception but at the many distractions put out by industry leaders. In the same way that the intelligent reader evaluates the cigarette advertisement which visually infers the good health and enjoyment of the attractive young couple sitting by a cool, clear flowing brook as it totally ignores the deadly implications of smoking, the *Wave 3* reader must remain aware of any written – or unwritten – warnings.

For example, in reading the story of one featured Nu Skin distributor who became a millionaire in just five years with a downline of over 5,000 strong, it is wise to absorb the revealing message of the footnote in which the author clarifies that "in no case did the distributors portrayed in the book represent to the author that their incomes were typical for the industry or their companies... On the contrary, the author selected interview subjects specifically for their outstanding achievements."

One could get caught up in the stories: the distributor who became a millionaire before the age of 30 as the head of Oxyfresh; one who earned $70,000 in just six months and along the way built a lasting network of new friends and associates; another who earned $100,000 in his first year and bought a 3,300-square foot home and a Mercedes SL sports car between vacations to Mexico and New Zealand.

The careful reader will find that interposed among these stories are some grim facts. While many of the success stories indicate that the time required to build incredible fortunes can be measured in months, we are informed that 99% of MLM companies themselves "spike and disappear in eight months."

Wave 3 presents the process of choosing an MLM company as an intelligent and professional one for mature people. Entering the MLM world is shown to be the result of a rational decision which is supported with business wisdom and experience. The would-be MLMer is advised to check a potential company's financial soundness by getting a D&B report on its credit worthiness, to call the Better Business Bureau for records of complaints and the State Attorney General's office for charges of fraud. In juxtaposition to these cautionary notes, *Wave 3* goes on to say that the reader should not be too strongly persuaded by evidence of complaints or fraud investigations by remarking, "Remember that controversy... can be one of the surest hallmarks of success." Thus, the level-headed advice about checking a company's credentials before joining, like the stark notices of danger in cigarette ads, is fully swept away by the presentation of recruitment of downline networks which yield huge monthly profits. No due diligence is suggested on behalf of best friends and relatives.

"One of the most common mistakes is to provide your prospect with too much information," *Wave 3* advises. "Most prospects don't want a detailed lecture on the strengths of your company. They just want to know whether it will survive. They don't need a doctoral dissertation on your product. They just want to know if people will buy it. And, in most cases, they are not much concerned about how the compensation plan works. They just want to know how much money they can make."

Finally putting aside any subjective experience, let's take a look at the big, future picture offered of MLM as the "primary distribution channel of the 21st century" the selling of which "will become a normal adjunct of every day conversation." Here *Wave 3* quotes the editor of *Success* magazine – which is cited as the only major business publication which actively endorses MLM – telling us that "selling will become a spiritual act – a new path to self actualization. In the pursuit of salesmanship, network marketers will develop mental and spiritual health."

Is this really our future? To consider the prophecy's plausibility, several objective facts must be weighed. In whatever manner the 21st century develops, MLM today constitutes only 1% of all retail sales. As to the rapid future economic expansion of MLM, the May, 1995 edition of *Home Office Computing* had this to say to its readers on the subject, "The rocket ship (growth) myth is often supported by a statement that 50 to 60 percent of all retail sales in the future will be made via network marketing. As Michael Marker, who himself is an active participant in network marketing, says, 'The 50 to 60 percent legend gets updated every 10 years. In the 1970s, we were told this would occur by 1980. In the 1980s, it was said to be expected by 1990. And now it's going to happen by the year 2000.'"

As for MLM's eventually encompassing all goods and services, one must be reminded that the product offerings of this system today are characteristically unregulated, untechnical fringe items sold by uninformed and untrained representatives often through wildly exaggerated claims of performance. It is even more difficult to measure MLM's true impact as many of its sales are attributable to filling the pipeline with inventories purchased by multiple layers of distributors each hoping to expand its downline organization. In fact, many of these sales are actually pyramid scheme entrance fees. With this awareness, it is appropriate to question whether or not these products would ever be purchased in the real market place in the absence of the incentive of misguided and deluded hopes of building a massive sales organization.

At the end of his book, Stephen Butterfield speculated about the future of MLM, noting that the system did appear to address some of the great sociological trends in America such as the new value placed on "high touch" business to balance the influence of high tech industry in our lives and the desire of millions for more personal freedom from the controls of big business. He concluded that Amway's answer to these national needs "was purely an illusion" and believed that Amway would continue to grow for a time but would eventually decline due to a fatal weakness, the weakness identified as the transparency of the real product. "The basic intelligence of the public is not so easily hypnotized. The whole edifice depends on the belief of the person on the bottom who just bought a (sales) kit. Once that person... sees that the system is based on a lie, it begins to fall apart."

In actuality and rather than positioning itself to take over the U.S. economy, the very legitimacy of the MLM system is continually being called into question not only by the government, the respected business establishment, press and media but by million of Americans who, due to experience either as enroller or potential enrollee, despise MLM, resenting the commercialism which is insinuated into their personal relationships and families lives and the personal pressure tactics that are used by most MLM recruiters.

Section IV
A Renewed Vision

Where Have We Been, Where Are We Going?

> *We can deceive our selves*
> *into thinking we are*
> *developing spirituality, when*
> *instead we are strengthening*
> *our egocentricity through*
> *spiritual techniques. This*
> *fundamental distortion may be*
> *referred to as spiritual*
> *materialism.*[44]
>
> — Chogyam Trungpa

A good deal of time has passed since the fateful meeting recounted in our Introduction between the bogus human resources recruiter and the accused dream buster, their ensuing debate making clear the economic and philosophical battle lines between pro- and anti-MLM forces. Yet, we have seen that the truly insidious aspects of the MLM system are revealed not in such heated disputes between strangers but rather in the warm embrace of those to whom we are closest.

It is there that the experience of being used is most deeply felt as friends, lovers, family, neighbors, fellow church members, employees, all are targeted for enrollment and investment solicitation in accordance with the MLM catechism and in order to fulfill the relentless mathematical requirements of pyramid expansion. No relationship is outside the MLM sell, no one sacred enough to be excused from the pitch. The inescapable and frequent result of these boundless downline conversion efforts is that

---

[44] Chogyam Trungpa, *Cutting Through Spiritual Materialism.* Boston: Shambhala Publs., Inc., 1973, pg. 3.

the fundamental values and benefits of relationships are irrevocably damaged.

The son no longer feels free to share unbridled interest in his career of choice because it does not echo his father's new MLM involvement. Church members no longer feel safe to confide in their minister about financial or personal problems for fear that their confidences may result in a sales pitch touting a cure-all for life's problems. Formerly loving family reunions turn into tension-filled events permeated with aggressive talk about enrollment, opportunity and income. Chiropractors, dentists and medical doctors routinely advise their patients to use vitamin and food supplements not just for the patients' physical health but to serve the financial well-being of the recommending professional. In some cases, the sacred doctor/client relationship is reduced to one of upline/downline.

In the passionate hopes, exaggerated rhetoric and proselytizing zeal of those who have been involved in MLM and pyramid schemes, we can see clear evidence of a widespread sometimes frantic quest for community, security and spiritual deliverance. Yet, because MLM has replaced such profound human pursuits with total emphasis on financial success, the results of involvement with this industry are often the ruinous and disappointing opposites of its prophecies.

In fact, economic security is weakened as millions lose their time and savings in age-old schemes which pull funds from the vast majority at the base of a pyramid to the tiny percentages at its peak. Spirituality is further obscured by the distractions and diversions of frenzied programs which foster endless enrollment, constant persuasion and materialistic obsession. Ultimately, community is destroyed through mercenary manipulation.

In that MLM offers not just a career or a job but puts forth an entire philosophy of life, it is set apart from all other business institutions in America. The complete truth about MLM and pyramid schemes is subtle, startling and pervasive. It is so all-encompassing that we have only begun to see the impact on our lives of this way of doing business in which all personal relationships are subjected to and transformed by the dynamics and qualities of sales.

We may give attention to the rantings and ravings of special interests and professional lobbyists about government corruption. We may disapprove of unconscionable attorneys who instigate litigation between spouses, employers and employees or exploit accidents, injury, disease and other human tragedy. We may castigate the media for productions that glorify heedless, impersonal sex and senseless violence which defile community life. Yet, we seem to be overlooking a societal element which is much closer to home, devaluing our culture and the quality of our lives with its singular urging for financial pursuit.

Today, the force of MLM resides comfortably within our homes, families and churches. While it has accumulated significant financial and political clout,[45] its real power and influence are imbedded in a prevailing philosophy, an idea, a dream that lies within our own hearts. And for this very reason, the MLM industry is able to demoralize us with its nihilistic gospel which proclaims that we have seen the end of economic opportunity, the futility of career planning, the uselessness of personal saving or

---

[45] The formidable political clout of the Amway Corporation, the largest of all MLM companies, is well-documented. Guest speakers at its annual conventions have included Ronald Reagan, George Bush and Bob Dole. Jay Van Andel and Richard De Vos, Amway's founders, served as Chairperson and Chairman of the Finance Committee of the National Republican Party. Former Secretary of Defense, Alexander Haig, served as Amway's consultant on international affairs. The U.S. Congresswoman from Charlotte, North Carolina, the home of Amway's largest distributor, Dexter Yager, is an Amway distributor and reportedly received one-half of all her campaign contributions from other Amway distributors. See "She Did It Amway" by Rachel Burstein and Kerry Lauderman in *Mother Jones* magazine, October, 1996 pp. 48-51.

investment and the folly of employment, offering itself as the only viable choice for a future of financial security and personal happiness.

In the Airplane pyramid scheme earlier dissected, we saw how players exploited personal relationships, defrauded one another and guilelessly proclaimed outrageous even dangerous nonsense. What was it that made these erstwhile honest, caring people take leave of their senses and ethics? Certainly the scheme promised wealth which excited greed, avarice and envy. But, there was more to it than that.

People were in the grip of the belief that wealth is God's sign of deliverance. The scheme promised to deliver this wealth naturally, without struggle or labor. And, for this promised redemption, all judgment was suspended. Suddenly, the only purpose for life was to win and gain through enrollment. It also confirmed a belief that all too many share – that wealth is necessary in order for our lives to have meaning, a perfect illustration of what author Marsha Sinetar calls "the sad, psychic relationship between self-worth and our monetary worth."

If not for the sake of personal success and financial reward, what is life's purpose? How do we define the American Dream if not in dollars? How do we express our freedom in terms other than economic?

To answer these questions requires that we investigate the mythological power which holds sway over the mind, soul and imagination of almost every American. This all-persuasive, seductive influence is often expressed in the idea of the American Dream, that great promise held out to the world offering every individual, regardless of background, rank or privilege, the opportunity to earn a livelihood and pursue happiness.

In recent times, the mythic promise of America has narrowed in scope for millions of its citizens. Fears of economic decline, corporate downsizing, globalization and a self-serving governmental bureaucracy have led many to view the pursuit of happiness as merely a prescription for achieving instant and redemptive wealth. Faith in America's great promise – the opportunity for each individual to develop his or her unique talents and interests – has diminished. Economic security rather than economic opportunity or creative self-expression is now the obsession of many.

In timely response, MLM has found this vein of mass apprehension and offered a tantalizing answer. Wealth can be achieved not through cultivating unique and special interests, not by pursuing talents and passions and not through contribution and service. It will be achieved by enrollment in a disciplined, multi-national franchise system which is typified by a well-worn highway crowded with millions of others following the same bright lights and garish signage toward the mirage of a gleaming pot of gold on the horizon. Personal exploration is neither encouraged nor allowed but, by taking this path, one is promised the support of a new family of enlightened winners who have beaten the economic system. Enrolling everyone you know, indeed, everyone you care for, is the only requirement for membership.

Even as MLM would have it otherwise, surely, we can acknowledge that we must not always be selling. If we are, there can be no time for loving, simple sharing, teaching or serving. And, if we choose to ignore this awareness, we invite life to become only a commercial marketplace where all interactions are, ultimately, buy/sell transactions. This is, by far, the most fearsome thought we face when attempting to evaluate the MLM-driven world. Fearsome because so many seem to have become blind to this fact. Even more fearsome because others simply cease to care about other aspects of life.

Do What You Love and Money Will Follow?

Fortunately, MLM is not the only voice that is addressing the shifting tide of faith and expectation in the American Dream. As corporations are being taught how to cultivate and affirm fundamental human needs, we can see a new set of values developing through which people are supported and encouraged to honor their uniqueness and their intuitions in choosing their life's work. Despite all and in the face of ongoing misadventures in the business world, we are seeing more people authentically seeking their true vocations rather than blindly offering up their talents to some promising yet unfulfilling career, corporation or quick money scheme.

Even here we must be alert to the overreaching power of the American myth which ties wealth to spirit. Frequently, the new path to vocational integrity is offered but the same old rewards for taking this path are promised as, once again, we are told that divinity will reward our spiritual quests – with money. It is, therefore, wise to remain leary of messages asserting that, if we pay attention to our innate values and talents, they will inevitably lead us to not only profound satisfaction but to financial success as well. This, we will discover, is no more true than MLM's prophecy that wealth invariably comes to those who envision it and metaphysically align with it.

In her book, *To Build The Life You Want, Create The Work You Love,* author Marsha Sinetar has explored the concept of each person having a unique vocation, a personal calling to do some special work in life that he or she is ideally qualified in talent and interest to do. In large part, this work was in sequel to her earlier book, *Do What You Love And The Money Will Follow,* the title of which echoed the New Age idea that wealth is the certain result of vocational integrity. In her newer work, Ms. Sinetar tells us plainly that this is not. Or, more correctly, not necessarily.

As we study Sinetar's books, despite their alluring titles, we see that they are far from financial formulas. Those who take the time to read *Do What You Love And The Money Will Follow* may be surprised to find little instruction about achieving financial success and a great deal about achieving spirituality in the process of work. Sinetar's books stand at the beginning of a new body of thought in the way that MLM represents the collapse of the old.

Sinetar describes three stages for succeeding in "right livelihood." The first calls for the intrepid psychological action of letting go and taking practical steps in a new direction. The second stage involves conjuring up the persistence and courage to stay with the new program or to simply invite in and wait for further intuition.

Then, at the point where one might think she is about to prophesy the big financial pay-off, Sinetar instead introduces the notion of "inner wealth." She offers as an illustration of inner wealth the experience of an inspiring man she had met who happily pursued his career in environmentalism even though earning only $5,000 a year.

Sinetar, however, makes clear the fact that she has "no quarrel with making money" as she explains to her readers "that part of my definition of a successful life involves having the means to provide for ourselves and those who depend on us." It's clearly the prioritization of spirituality, self, work and money that can serve to give us pause.

The last thirty pages of *Do What You Love And The Money Will Follow*, as well as the concluding chapter of its sequel, *To Build The Life You Want, Create The Work You Love*,[46] are eloquent

---

[46] Marsha Sinetar, *Do What You Love And The Money Will Follow.* New York: Dell Publishing, 1987. *To Build The Life You Want, Create The Work You Love,* New York: St. Martin's Griffin, 1995.

explorations of the relationship of work to spirituality. Sinetar identifies a central truth that "work, done rightly, affords the individual an understanding of the key principles of life and of the Universe..." Indeed, in her books, Marsha Sinetar adds to a growing body of thought that is finally beginning to separate spirituality from financial success. In other words, money cannot be guaranteed to follow doing what you love.

Armies of brilliant, never-to-be-discovered actors, talented painters whose years of work will only be seen at weekend art festivals, passionate but unpublished writers, small business people overwhelmed by Walmarts, down-sized white collar managers and unemployed craftsmen may never earn great sums of money. Yet, they are not out of tune with the Infinite and many, indeed, love what they do.

Talent, new ideas, services or efficiencies are sometimes rewarded in a healthy market economy but often they are not. Just as the market resists predictability, the spirituality of work is certainly not reducible to formulas. As the wise old Indian chief said in the movie *Little Big Man*, "Sometimes the magic does not work." In facing this truth, however, we will begin to see our power.

Not to be mourned then is the passing of the need for the spiritual quick fix or the taunts of a Deepak Chopra who promises that "You can change your life more effortlessly, more efficiently, more rapidly than you can change your clothes."[47] Efficiency and effortlessness no longer need be associated with spirituality. Thus, the New Age notion that spirituality can be managed with business-like rigor so we can get on with other areas of our lives, like going on vacation, is dissipating.

---

[47] Nightingale-Conant 1996 promotional literature advertising "Magical Mind, Magical Body" audio tapes by Deepak Chopra.

Thankfully, spirituality is being rediscovered not as the goal that Chopra goes on to offer in his advertisements for magical audio tapes but more as a lifelong process. As Sinetar finally recommends, "Heed what you genuinely need and value, here and now... Bit by intelligible bit, make choices that honor your healthiest instincts, your noble desire. This is how we build a life."

MLM and pyramid schemes promise a short cut to this fundamental process, a magical detour which allegedly wins us the so-called prizes of life – leisure and high income. After these are accomplished and if we are still interested in a life of our own making, they tell us, we can easily make this a pursuit as one might take up a hobby after retirement. In actuality, most followers of this prescription get lost in the detour and for years lose even the vaguest memory of their original dreams.

Many are now discovering that it is our mission to build a life – not just "get a life" or create a lifestyle – and that our uniquely-considered work is elemental to building that real life.

Searching for Meaning, Again

The spark that ignited New Thought in America and laid a foundation for today's New Age thinking came from Ralph Waldo Emerson's recognition of the sterility and emptiness of 19th century New England Unitarianism. His writings along with those of a small visionary group that came to be called Transcendentalists sought to raise the spirits and renew the vision of America with a message of personal freedom and exalted individualism. In their view, traditional faith had been overtaken by cold scientific materialism and ever-expanding commercialism. True spirituality was being extinguished, leaving empty ritual and moral hypocrisy in its path.

In example, we can see that, similarly, after having been largely absorbed into the mainstream culture, New Age doctrine has largely lost its power to transform spirit or community. The movement now seems morally challenged and intellectually confused, its infirmity clearly seen in the ease with which illegal pyramid schemes and MLMs are able to capitalize upon its precepts and infiltrate its community. The current day result is that the acquisitive materialism of western culture has captured the hearts of even New Agers leaving only a thin veneer of disingenuous spirituality which cleverly and temptingly equates wealth with salvation.

If we are able to acknowledge the coldness, the hollowness of the current materially-based version of spirituality, it will probably dawn on many of us that we have simply arrived at another time for renewal and re-creation. At this juncture, we may find that, as is often the case in suffering the evaluation of life's dilemmas, the traumatic call to investigate the world of MLM and pyramid schemes has beneficially unveiled the emptiness of prosperity consciousness as it is presently perceived.

In the void that follows such a disclosure, we will likely be faced with that personally terrifying but nonetheless worthwhile question, "Is there a better way and, if so, what is it?" Even more challenging to address is the fact that for many who have been profoundly disappointed in or even duped by an MLM or pyramid scheme encounter, this question seems too painful to even raise.

However, if we can begin to realize that it was probably in our most vulnerable moments that we tried to believe that salvation could come from a system which was actually designed to cheat many more people than it could reward, we can advance. If we acknowledge that it was our fear that turned us into victims, misplaced faith that led us to abandon our sure knowledge that prosperity is about far more than having a lot of money and, ultimately, that our greed became not only engaged but actually took the lead in the process – well, then all is truly not lost.

We had listened for signs and direction in audio tapes from prophets of global trends. As we quested for prosperity, we had turned for encouragement to the hopeful messages of countless motivational speakers and positive-thinking seminar leaders. We had sought guidance and salvation in the charts of astrologers who predict the coming of the Aquarian Age. Yet, with all our continuing and grasping desire for quick and complete answers to the riddles of life, they seem to have eluded us. Once again, we are encouraged to return to the matter of what it is that we are daily attempting to learn and live.

However, in trying to simplify our quest, confusion can still arise. If, for instance, we are to assume that it is success that we are after, we must begin by defining its standard so as to know if and when we have achieved it. In looking at popular characterizations of success towards achieving the goal of clarification, we run into odd little interpretations like that of self-actualization guru, Anthony Robbins. He says, "My definition of success is to use your life in a way that causes you to feel tons of pleasure and very little pain...Someone who has achieved a lot but is living in emotional pain...isn't truly successful."[48] More pleasure than pain – that's success? Well, maybe not. Fortunately, many of us have come too far along the spiritual path to believe, even momentarily, that our life's work could possibly be about chasing pleasure and avoiding pain.

Regarding success, perhaps it is the natural state of the universe, as one of the more popular MLMs regularly states in its marketing literature. But then so is failure for all of its learning purposes. And despite the fact that the need for money keeps rearing its demanding head, there are significant numbers of people who truly believe that one's life work is only meaningful if it is connected in some way to further spiritual enlightenment. In actuality, all this causes us to know is that there are two profound areas of spirituality that can, through further search, be advanced – the spiritual nature of work in our lives and our relationship to money.

Particularly for those who believed most fully that MLM was the answer to that lost job or career, the one and only way to truly become wealthy and happy, the absolute answer to a lifetime of dreams and for those who have, for the moment, given up hope – we urge you to read on so that you might reconsider the results of your experience towards a further enlightened view.

---

[48] Anthony Robbins, *How to Really Get What You Want, Awaken the Giant Within*. New York: Simon and Schuster, 1992.

False Profits

Beyond Self-Improvement: Caring for the Soul

"If you set out to be less than you are capable of being, I warn you, you will be deeply unhappy for the rest of your life."
— *Abraham Maslow*

Our study of MLM and pyramid schemes has made it painfully clear that countless people along the way lost faith in themselves and gave it to money. Even clearer is that, as a result, vast numbers of people were easily lured away from any inclination to determine their true callings. These examinings allow us to see how spiritually bereft many became of those who were involved with MLM. They can also serve to awaken us to a message that Marianne Williamson delivered in her early lectures on *A Course in Miracles*. In the late 1980's, Williamson spoke passionately about the forces of spirituality and materialism both of which were accelerating in the approach to the new millennium. A challenge was issued to those who so aspired to pour even greater effort into achieving the dream of a spiritually advanced society in deflection of its current most worldly character.

While we have no knowledge of what kind of wealth might result from the honoring of such dreams, one promise that can certainly be made is that any such contributions will significantly add to the betterment of our world. Ultimately, they may further lead us to see that faith in a destiny of wealth is not required to have a rich and fulfilling life. In fact, the very idea of any result or reward for our integrity, affirmations, visualizations and meditations may fade away to be replaced by something more enduring and far more personal.

Ultimately, we may come to the same conclusion as the alchemists who finally determined that the true philosopher's stone, instead of being an element which could turn lead into gold, was a far more significant power which resides within each one of us.

But, what if underneath it all we simply do not know what to do with ourselves? Author Barbara Sher wrote in her book, *I Could Do Anything If I Only Knew What It Was*[49], "Not knowing what you want to do with your life is no joke. It's painful to be without direction." However, let us immediately dispel the notion that this is a time to despair one's not knowing. Rather it is a time to reconnoiter and consider the fact that Sher, in meeting with hundreds of people to hear their stories, found this. "It had never occurred to them that down deep they really knew what they wanted but their desires were masked by an inner conflict. Knowing the problem came as a great surprise – and a great relief...." Sher continued, "This book is designed to help you find the good life. By that, I don't mean swimming pools, mansions and private jets – unless those are really your big passions. But if you picked up (this) book... you're probably looking for a lot more than a swimming pool. You want a life you will love."

Just what does that mean? Well, Sher went on to tell us that, in the 1980s, two Harvard psychologists completed a study of people who called themselves happy. There were two things that this group of people shared and they did not include money, success, health or love. What these fulfilled people all held in common was that they knew exactly what they wanted and they felt they were moving toward getting it. Sher tells us plainly, "That's what makes life feel good: when it has direction, when you are headed straight for what you love." While this

---

[49] Barbara Sher with Barbara Smith, *I Could Do Anything If I Only Knew What It Was*. New York: Delacorte Press, 1994.

sounds a lot like work of the heart and soul, a special kind of living and the very least we should be doing for ourselves, many of us simply are not.

Keeping Your Best Interests in Mind and Heart

Inherent in the human condition is the fact that taking care of ourselves does not always come naturally. That's why we are encouraged to find people who can not only help us to find our way to the things we love but keep us moving in the right direction. In response to the fact that many people do not have ready access to such positive, clear-minded and individualized help, a new breed of professionals has emerged, represented by those who are dedicating themselves to supporting individuals in meeting the great challenge of building authentic lives. These people are called coaches.

Born out of the competitive pressures of today's economy as well as the struggle to find balance in the frenzied pace of modern life, the new coaching profession is earning devotees not only among CEOs, entrepreneurs, professionals and people in career transition but with countless others who are grappling with life issues.

Thomas Leonard, a leading figure in this new profession, has coached more than 600 clients in his career, started Coach University, a national training and resource center for coaching, and has been featured extensively in the media as the person behind the coaching movement. A profession in its earliest stages of development, it is estimated that there are over a thousand full-time coaches across the country most of whom work individually with their clients over the telephone in weekly one-hour sessions.

"Coaches develop a personal partnership with their clients that is very different from the relationship people have with a therapist, a consultant or even a friend," says Leonard, a former accountant and financial planner. "The client uses the coach to set goals, grow, get a great life and make changes, and one of the reasons it works is that a coach helps a client stay in action. A coach is like a still small voice saying, 'Are you really doing what you want to do?'"[50]

Artful Living

The clear point is that, however we manage to find it, we all have a purpose and, our primary job beyond unearthing it is to find its proper expression towards living a passionate, meaningful and heartfelt life. Here, perhaps author of NY Times bestseller *Care of the Soul*,[51] Thomas Moore can add a bit of encouragement and guidance to the process. He writes, "We can now return to one of Plato's expressions for care of the soul – *techne tou biou*, the craft of life. Care of the soul requires craft – skill, attention and art. To live with a high degree of artfulness means to attend to the small things that keep the soul engaged in whatever we are doing and is the very heart of soul-making. From some grand overview of life, it may seem that only the big events are ultimately important. But to the soul, the most minute details and the most ordinary activities, carried out with mindfulness and art, have an effect far beyond their apparent insignificance."

Moore goes on to offer his explanation of why even those who have them in great quantity come to realize that success, money and all manner of material possessions alone do not ensure happiness. "As long as we leave care of the soul out of our daily

---

[50] Full information about this new profession can be found on the CoachU home page on the World Wide Web, http://www.coachu.com/info.htm. The new business of coaching was featured in the February 5, 1996 edition of *Newsweek, p. 48.*

[51] Thomas Moore, *Care of the Soul, a Guide for Cultivating Depth and Sacredness in Everyday Life.* New York: Harper Collins, 1992.

lives, we will suffer the loneliness of living in a dead, cold, unrelated world. We can 'improve' ourselves to the maximum and yet we will still feel the alienation inherent in a divided existence. We will continue to exploit nature and our capacity to invent new things, but both will continue to overpower us, if we do not approach them with enough depth and imagination.

"The way out of this neurosis is to leave our modern divisions behind and learn from other cultures, from art and religion and from new movements in philosophy that there is another way to perceive the world. We can replace our modernist psychology with care of the soul and we can begin building a culture that is sensitive to matters of the heart."

If this should sound like too other-worldly an approach, let's take a look at what Tony Schwartz, author of the NY Times bestseller, *Trump: The Art of the Deal*, has to say about the importance of worldly success. After documenting the life and philosophy of one of America's most flamboyant money-makers and extravagant spenders, Schwartz wrote in a subsequent book, *What Really Matters: Searching for Wisdom in America*[52], "In 1988, I co-authored a book with Donald Trump called *The Art of the Deal* which became an enormous commercial success and provided me with the recognition that I had been seeking for many years as a journalist.

"Now that I had 'arrived' professionally, I finally had financial security along with a good marriage, healthy children, good friends and an active, involved lifestyle. So with all the puzzle pieces of the American Dream in place, why wasn't I happier? Eventually, I realized that beyond succeeding in work and building a comfortable life with my family and friends, I lacked the experience of meaning. I realized that no external source of achievement or

---

[52] Tony Schwartz, *What Really Matters: Searching for Wisdom in America.* New York: Bantam Books, 1995.

relationship could provide lasting happiness and inner security,... I set out on a five-year search for a more complete life, an experience of my own essence, which I came to call wisdom." Later Schwartz stated in other words much the same philosophy that Moore espouses in *Care of the Soul* when he said, "We remain alienated from our essence if we fill ourselves up with work, relationships, sports and entertainment..."

Even as we move away from the notion that money or all other manner of external possessions are the best rewards and get comfortable with the fact that we need to attend to our inner workings at a much more intimate level, we, once again, run into the problem of how and where we are going to do this all-important work. Perhaps we feel disappointed at every turn, our hopes critically wounded in the process. And, just where does all this leave us – with merely the hope of some future enlightenment? Hardly a rousing prospect, especially in light of today's cynical view of hope as some deluded, disempowered state of mind.

As an aside and while remembering the assurance that out of every season of grief comes learning and renewed hope, we may just wish to take a moment to reconsider our definition of hope in light of these words from author Joan Borysenko. In her book, *Fire in the Soul* she says, "Hope is a form of blessing. To bless is to increase, to allow something to unfold in its fullness. To hope is to create a sacred space, a space of possibility, in which the goodness of the Universe can express itself. The stance we adopt in that sacred space is one of readiness, openness and non-attachment to a particular outcome." Not only does this sound interestingly close to the original definition of prosperity before it was redefined as simply getting rich but it clears a way for us to continue with our dreams as it urges us to participate in and encourage change in some very vital aspects of American life.

In returning to Thomas Moore's *Care of the Soul*, we can see how much of a bellwether work this is as it signals a movement back to individual contribution and personal expression. Moore began this book with the assertion that the "great malady of the twentieth century, implicated in all of our troubles and affecting us individually and socially, is loss of soul." His work, he writes, "offers a philosophy for soulful living... without striving for perfection or salvation."

Offering a contemplative examination of the state of spirituality in our culture, Moore – who spent most of his youth studying for the Roman Catholic priesthood in a monastery – modeled *Care of the Soul* on a self-help book from the Middle Ages. And, despite the fact that it is filled with esoteric discussions of medieval mysticism and classical mythology, this book remained on the *New York Times* Bestseller List for well over a year.

Moore contrasts his book with the great mass of self-help literature of our times which contains an unspoken but clear salvational tone, implying that if we could only learn to be assertive, loving, angry, expressive, contemplative or thin, our troubles would be over. It would have surprised no one if *rich* had been included on Moore's recounted list of popular prescriptions for salvation.

Like Marsha Sinetar, Moore reminds us that all work is a vocation, "a calling from a place that is the source of meaning and identity, the roots of which lie beyond human intention and interpretation... All work is sacred, whether you are building a road, cutting a person's hair, or taking out the garbage... Therefore, finding the right work is like discovering your own soul."

Moore sees our current detachment from our work reflected in projections of inordinate value on the money our work produces and in our lack of attention to any moral sense of our work or, as he puts it, making money a fetish rather than a medium with which we interact with our world. "It is not possible to care for the soul while violating or disregarding our own moral sensibility," Moore writes as he envisions a society that focuses more on soulful work rather than on maximum profits.

We are not, however, saying that regaining a sense of pride and finding our own souls in our work, or, courageously pursuing our vocations assures us of enough money on which to live. Practical judgments about making a living must still be made. But, judgment in matters of money and work will be framed and guided by our beliefs, our sense of self worth and our sense of connectedness with the world. Ultimately, these are spiritual matters. Thomas Moore notes that when concern for profit is split from work's inherent value, "pleasure in money cannot take the place of pleasure in work... In most work there can be a close relationship between caring for the world in which we live... and caring for the quality of our way of life."

Moore simply returns us to the challenge of synthesizing spirituality with material life. "Perhaps our madly consumerist society," he speculates, "is showing signs of runaway tendencies toward an abstract and intellectualized approach to life... The cure of materialism then would be to find concrete ways of getting soul back into... our physical engagements with the world."

The pathway to bringing our souls back into our daily world, advises Moore, is not through more external spiritual activity but by paying much closer attention to our inner life. This is a contemplative, deeply personal process that may include noting our dreams, our deepest longings and our highest ideals and then honoring them with our commitments and actions.

This stands in stark contrast to a world that dangles $50,000-a-month incomes, testimonials of BMW owners and assurances of ease and efficiency in attaining wealth and spirituality. It also offers a far different guide than the one presented by prophets of fear and insecurity who tell us our dreams are foolish and impractical while offering us their own foolproof ways to gain wealth.

Perhaps it is the healthy sense of skepticism which scientist Carl Sagan[53] encouraged us to develop that can, ultimately, help us redefine unfortunate past experiences as they relate to our future dreams beginning with these three characteristics:
* The willingness to change views.
* A discipline of testing out new ideas.
* The courage to face and embrace the less than pleasant.

Adopting a philosophy of positive and healthy skepticism will take bravery, for the purveyors of instant gratification swarm all around us. They promise salvation, wealth, ecstasy, love and immortality. They claim to hold great and profound secrets that can be learned only through the surrender of reason and will. We are told that we must simply believe. Yet, just one little ounce of Carl Sagan's skepticism or what Thomas Moore calls "faith which allows uncertainty" could have saved thousands from the financial and moral disasters we have herein recounted.

An Awakening Corporate America

One reason many people have lost faith in themselves and given up the pursuit of their dreams is that they perceive less and less opportunity in the established business world of America. The devastating impact of the sudden firings of hundreds of thousands of people by some of the nation's premier corporations led *Newsweek* magazine to put on its cover the photos of some of America's best known CEOs under the headline, "Corporate Killers." A better title might have been Dream Killers. For the greatest impact of these layoffs is not economic although this is not to be diminished. Rather, the impact is psychological,

---

[53] Carl Sagan, "The Burden of Skepticism" in *Not Necessarily the New Age*. Buffalo: Prometheus Books, 1988, pp. 361-372.

even spiritual and it has demoralized and terrorized many people.

However, mass firings in American big business do not by any means fully or even typically characterize the reality of industry today. It is not reasonable to write off the nation's larger corporations as if they no longer exist as places of opportunity. There actually are noble and transformational movements underway in the larger business world that support people's creativity or the pursuit of personal expression and contribution. And, it is the companies who are attempting to embrace this thinking that must be encouraged and pursued.

Prime among those who have set out to transform the American workplace is W. Edwards Deming.[54] Most Japanese business and government leaders credit Dr. Deming's philosophy and training with the global leadership of Japanese manufacturing. His work represents a cohesive and comprehensive new philosophy, one which entire companies are striving to learn and adopt.

Deming's view represents the larger movement toward greater value placed on the individual's contribution to the company. His system discourages manipulation and contrived competition with pay incentives. He teaches that pride in workmanship and opportunity to powerfully contribute and improve a company are far more authentic drives. In his teachings, we see the sense of vocation honored and a call for a new relationship between work and money.

In Deming's sweeping new vision of American industry, corporations put their people first and strive for quality and contribution to the economy

---

[54] For information on the teachings of W. Edwards Deming contact Massachusetts Institute of Technology, Center for Advanced Educational Services, Cambridge, MA 02139. E-mail: caes-courses@mit.edu. Also refer to http://www.caes.mit.edu/products/deming/home.html on the World Wide Web.

ahead of short term profits. For example, in Deming's representational future:

- It is no longer acceptable to dump employees onto the heap of the unemployed.
- Long-term commitment to new learning and new philosophy is required by management that seeks transformation... people who expect quick results are doomed to disappointment.
- Management must understand barriers on the job that rob the hourly worker of his birthright, the right to pride of workmanship.

Another voice that is advocating the transformation of businesses into organizations where individuals can express their callings and positively contribute is that of entrepreneur and visionary writer, John Renesch. Editor of *Rediscovering the Soul of Business, Community Building, New Traditions in Business* and *The New Bottom Line*, Renesch's works acknowledge that the old paternalistic corporations such as IBM are dying away. Like Dr. Deming, he addresses the urgent need for a new model of corporate responsibility, one which engages each person's creativity and ability to contribute to the overall organization.

Renesch's newsletter, *The New Leaders* features contributions from M. Scott Peck, Thomas Moore and Amatai Etzioni, all writers who are working towards the transformation of the business world by addressing the loss of confidence and sense of declining opportunity in the traditional workplace. In the July/August, 1995 edition of his newsletter, Renesch wrote, "Barely half way through the year, we have seen an explosion of interest in doing business in a way that nurtures the human spirit, reunites us with our souls... Are we collectively telling ourselves that it is time...to go to work every day with our hearts and souls as well as our minds and bodies?" As if in answer to himself, Renesch concluded, "We have an opportunity with this new found popularity of 'soulful' discussion... to give freedom to our souls or to further indulge our egos. It's a choice each of us can make on our own."[55]

So, we begin to see that W. Edwards Deming, John Renesch, Thomas Moore, Marsha Sinetar, Barbara Sher, Tony Schwartz, Thomas Leonard and countless others are reflecting a new set of values that build upon the past without promising a specified and unrealistic result other than the personal fulfillments that are experienced as part of life's process. They each are teaching a different way of being, a humbler approach, as Thomas Moore would say – one that will bind us all more tightly together as a working society.

---

[55] *New Leaders Press*, 1668 Lombard St., San Francisco, CA 94123. Tel. (415) 928-1473, Fax (415)928-3346.

Beyond Prosperity:
Spirituality and Community

One of the revelations that followed this study is just how much so many of us have in common particularly with regard to the spiritual search. The various MLM and pyramid scheme encounters herein discussed make it clear that the metaphysically enlightened, philosophically elite, the shrewd and the naive were all wandering in the same desert, pursuing the mundane and the material all the while starving for the spiritual and the profound.

After labeling our lives inadequate and our work unsatisfactory, many of us abandoned our more traditional beginnings as we looked for spirituality in our huddled little MLM masses. We did not find it. We sought the benefits of prosperity through pyramid schemes and found ruin or, at least, shame. Where, then, can we find the fulfillments of life? Right where we are – albeit in the presence of some challenging realities.

"Life is difficult," wrote M. Scott Peck in *The Road Less Traveled*, [56] a book that has remained on the *New York Times* Bestseller List for well over a decade. "This is a great truth... because once we truly see this truth, we transcend it. Once we truly know that life is difficult – once we truly understand and accept it – then life is no longer difficult. Because once it is accepted, the fact that life is difficult no longer matters.

"Most do not fully see this truth that life is difficult. Instead they moan more or less incessantly, noisily or subtly, about the enormity of their problems, their burdens and their difficulties as if life were generally easy, as if life *should* be easy."

---

[56] M. Scott Peck, *The Road Less Traveled*. New York: Touchstone, Simon and Schuster, Inc., 1978.

We cannot say where the original and faulty notion that life should be easy originated. However, it is painfully clear to see the lengths to which millions of people have gone to prove – or disprove, as the case may be – that this highly-prized life of ease can, indeed, be achieved through MLM or pyramid schemes. There are a few who have achieved their purpose, countless more who have not.

We know that the lure of money is the most powerful tool in the MLM arsenal. In the final assessment, we think that while money is certainly a primary goal, there is another compelling factor which not only attracts people but keeps them from letting go of the MLM world. That factor, we believe, is a deep-seated need for community.

As with the Airplane Game, the search was spiritually based, the horror realized only when the greed became too apparent to ignore. Yet, even then, many hung on simply unable to relinquish the dream that the scheme had awakened. They had become a society with a goal and no one willingly let go of the exhilaration that was so much a part of their community of friends. Even when the confusion about spirituality and prosperity as it related to the scheme surfaced, the more important goal became to hold the community together. One could easily ask why.

Perhaps, Scott Peck gave us the answer in another of his opening lines, this one from his 1987 offering, *The Different Drum*.[57] "Community is currently rare." Maybe in the combining of Peck's two thoroughly striking points, we can embrace another truth, one which can serve to free us to continue our own life's work in loving communion with our fellow sojourners: *Life is most difficult without community.*

This, then, is where our final searchlight will fall, on America's lack of and desire for community.

---

[57] M. Scott Peck, *The Different Drum: Community Making and Peace.* New York: Touchstone, Simon and Schuster, Inc., 1987.

After his pithy opening, Peck continued, "The seeds of community reside in humanity – a social species – just as a gem originally resides in the earth. But it is not yet a gem, only a potential one. So it is that geologists refer to a gem in the rough simply as a stone. A group becomes a community in somewhat the same way that a stone becomes a gem – through a process of cutting and polishing. Once cut and polished it is something beautiful...

"The gem of community is so exquisitely beautiful it may seem unreal to you, like a dream you once had when you were a child, so beautiful it may seem unattainable. As Gellah and his co-authors put it, the notion of community 'may also be resisted as absurdly Utopian, as a project to create a perfect society, but the transformation of which we speak is both necessary and modest. Without it, indeed, there may be very little future to think about at all.'[58] The problem is that the lack of community is so much the norm in our society, one without experience would be tempted to think, How could we possibly get there from here? It *is* possible; we *can* get there from here. Remember that to the uninitiated eye it would seem impossible for a stone ever to become a gem."

We as individuals crave spirituality and prosperity. We as a nation hunger for community. As a result, untold numbers of people have been waylaid by MLM or pyramid schemes with their unrealistic promises and their very misuse of community. Sadly, it often takes tragedy to witness real community, the kind of unconditional pulling together we have seen after such devastating events as the Oklahoma City bombing and Hurricane Andrew in South Florida. More recently after Raleigh-Durham had been laid to waste by Hurricane Fran, business establishments published

---

[58] Robert Bellah, et al., *Habits of the Heart.* Berkeley: Univ. of California Press, 1985, p. 286.

messages of assurance and support, offering the community beds and other necessary furniture through deeply-deferred payment plans. Carolina Power and Light issued continuing and, literally, empowering news with a community count-down as customers received restored service. It is this kind of community most of us are deeply desirous of, absent of the tragedy, free from blackmail or false promises or profits.

Looking at our world today, it might appear that greed and materialism are winning. Further, it might seem in this study of MLM and pyramid schemes that there is the germ of a notion that we, as spiritual people, should not seek wealth or prosperity. To the contrary, we can be owners of great wealth. But, let us consider re-establishing the idea that with great wealth, as with great talent or ability, there comes a responsibility to the world. If we are not in search of the spiritual life, these principles clearly have no meaning. But for those who are seeking a more faithful life, the search for prosperity will more than likely carry much less importance than adherence to the spiritual mission. Our needs for community – our desires for comfort – our longings for security and affection – all these worthy things will fall in comfortable order of priority when viewed through our spiritual lens.

In the end, perhaps the new road into the future is not another beautifully paved highway that promises gold and white light on the horizon but a humbler and rougher path that quietly suggests that our quest will be satisfied through honoring ourselves and others along the way. As we deepen our awareness of what it means to be prosperous, spiritual human beings, we may just find that the answer to peaceful, spiritual living remains, as always, in the attention we pay to the joy and gratitude that can be summoned in response to each new day of learning.

Authors

Robert L. Fitzpatrick is an advocate and spokesman for new spiritual and social values in the realms of church, government, business and personal life. Reared as a devout Roman Catholic, at the age of eighteen Fitzpatrick entered a Catholic seminary to study for the priesthood. Not finding enough relevance to the great social issues of the 1960s in the seminary curriculum caused him to leave his theological studies to take up sociology.

Research into urban social problems led Fitzpatrick to Chicago to study the controversial community action techniques and philosophy of the nationally-acclaimed urban organizer, Saul D. Alinsky. Carrying the philosophy and techniques he learned in Alinsky's training program, Fitzpatrick returned to his conservative southern hometown of Charlotte, North Carolina, where he organized a network of neighborhood associations, senior citizen groups and taxpayer organizations. After six years of challenging the old political and business establishment of Charlotte on the subjects of neighborhood preservation, school construction, mass transit, airport expansion and increased citizen involvement in government decision making, Fitzpatrick's work led directly to the restructuring of Charlotte's elected body of government to a fairer and more representative district system.

Urban activism and community development provided the foundation for Fitzpatrick's later successful career as a nationally recognized expert in industrial relations. He has started and organized two national trade associations; his articles on new models for distribution in mature industries have appeared in trade journals for graphic arts, sanitation supply, automobile parts, office automation, wholesale florist, materials handling and food processing industries, among others and have been reprinted in four languages. His advanced concepts on dealer/manufacturer partnership have been largely adopted in the United States by the graphics systems division of Fuji Photo Film, the fastest growing supplier of digital and photographic imaging products in America.

In Brasschaat, Belgium and Guadalajara, Mexico, Fitzpatrick has organized international symposia on distributor/manufacturer relations that have attracted industry leaders from over 25 countries. He regularly publishes THE EAGLE, an international journal for industry leaders in the graphic arts industry, and serves as special consultant to several national trade associations. His consulting client list includes Fuji Photo, DuPont, Polaroid, Mitsubishi and AB Dick, among others.

An avid student of New Thought philosophy and a graduate of several personal development and enlightenment courses, he has spent much of his life reflecting on the connections between what we believe and what we manifest.

Robert L. Fitzpatrick lives in Charlotte, North Carolina with his wife and soulmate, Terry Thirion, who is a personal success coach trained by CoachU. He continues his writing, public speaking, consulting work and his spiritual pilgrimage of inquiry.

Joyce K. Reynolds is a writer, corporate trainer and speaker who has devoted her recent career to encouraging the concept of service and the growth of spirituality in the workplace.

Having lived all over America as a result of career pursuits, Reynolds left her last corporate position as Senior Vice President of Marketing for a New York City-based international communications firm in 1986 to pursue her entrepreneurial interests. Her first company, Retail Advertising Video Enterprises, Inc. (R.A.V.E.), was responsible for creating and producing benchmark programming in the category of special interest films primarily for the direct marketing industry.

A former radio talk show host, Reynolds continues to facilitate entrepreneurship through a private coaching practice which grew out of her weekly radio segment, *On My Own.* Author of such corporate training programs as Responsibilities in the Workplace, Reynolds focuses this work on equality, the development of open communications and the enhancement of ethical business practices with emphasis on the subject of sexual harassment. She is a keynote speaker in the business and spiritual communities.

Joyce K. Reynolds earned a B.S. degree with a major in Sociology and a minor in Music from her beloved alma mater, Indiana University, and recently moved from New York City to Fort Lauderdale, Florida.

False Profits

Index

PV -- POINT VALUES

BV -- BUSINESS VALUES

AMO -- AMWAY MOTIVATIONAL ORGINIZATION

MLM - MULTILEVEL MARKETING AND
     ASSOCIATED ILLEGAL PYRAMID
     SCHMES

AMWAY NOW QUIXTAR

To Order Additional Copies

FALSE PROFITS
Robert L. Fitzpatrick and Joyce K. Reynolds

Complete and Send the Following Information:

Name_____

Address_____

City _____ State _____ Zip _____

Tel. (_____)_____

No. Of Copies _____

Ordering Options (check one):

___ Send form with check

___ Fax form with credit card info: (704)334-0220

___ Call toll-free to order only: 1-888-334-2047

___ E-mail: FalsProfts@aol.com

___ Contact your local bookstore: ISBN 0-9648795-1-4

Credit Card:

_____ Visa _____ MC _____ AMEX ____ Discover

Card Number _____

Name on Card _____

Exp. Date_____ / _____

Signature _____

Price: $12.95 plus $3.50 shipping per book
Sales tax: Please add 6% for books shipped to FL and NC
Shipped: First-class priority

Mail and Make Check Payable:
Herald Press
1235-E East Blvd. #101   Charlotte, NC 28203

Visit our World Wide Web Site:
http://www.FalseProfits.com